The GAY COUPLE'S GUIDE *to* WEDDING PLANNING

Dedication

This book is dedicated to Armand Scala,
the best husband I never had.
All my love, always.

Published by Sellers Publishing, Inc.

Copyright © 2012 Sellers Publishing, Inc.
Text © 2012 David Toussaint
Photography © 2012 Melanie Wesslock (www.melaniewesslock.com)
except where noted: cover (left corner), and on pages 55, 76, 142, and 149 are copyright
© ArrowStudio, LLC for Shutterstock. The photos on pages 14, 15, 32, 37, 46, 56, 57, 66,
67, 72, 86, 93, 95, 101, 102, 104, 105, 120, 134, 138, 145, 146, and 151 are copyright ©
Kathempel Photography (www.kathempel.com). The photo on page 48 is copyright © Cathy
MacNeill. The photo of Joey Gonzalez that appears on pages 19, 49, 59, 66, 85, 98, 107,
121, 133, 141, 146, and 151 is copyright © Kurt R. Brown. The photo of the author that
appears on the back cover of the book is copyright © Piero Ribelli (www.pieroribelli.com).

Sellers Publishing, Inc.
161 John Roberts Road, South Portland, Maine 04106
Visit our Web site: www.sellerspublishing.com • E-mail: rsp@rsvp.com

ISBN: 978-1-4162-0849-5
e-ISBN: 978-1-4162-0862-4

Library of Congress Control Number: 2012931620

10 9 8 7 6 5 4 3 2 1

Printed and bound in China.

The GAY COUPLE'S GUIDE *to* WEDDING PLANNING

EVERYTHING GAY MEN NEED TO KNOW TO CREATE A FUN, ROMANTIC, AND MEMORABLE CEREMONY

by DAVID TOUSSAINT

Photographs by Melanie Wesslock *and* Katje Hempel

SELLERS PUBLISHING

CONTENTS

INTRODUCTION

A few years ago, someone asked me why I thought I was qualified to write about gay weddings. I'm not married, and he didn't think a single man had the know-how. At the time, I'd written one book on the topic, and I'd written for a couple of wedding sites — gay and straight — as well as eight years for *Brides*® magazine. In fact, my 2003 article on same-sex marriage for *Brides* was historic — it was the first time any major bridal publication had featured a story on this subject.

The question about my qualifications is certainly valid, and I have a two-part answer. First, I believe I'm more than qualified to write about gay weddings because, in addition to my extensive experience covering them, the subject increasingly enthralls me with every couple I speak to and with every fairy-tale romance I see come true. Growing up in suburban California, I saw a lot of weddings, but I didn't always see ceremonies that were filled with love. If I didn't have my own love affair with same-sex nuptials, I would have abandoned the topic long ago.

Second, as for me being unmarried, in some ways that's why I'm even more qualified. I choose to be single because I've yet to find the man I'm convinced I want to spend the rest of my life with. As an old-fashioned guy, I still believe that's the only reason to have a wedding, legal or otherwise. Yes, I've been in love, and yes, I've come close to saying those vows. I could whip up a wedding in my sleep, but that's not the point.

A wedding is the beginning of a commitment that takes work, and marriage, is not to be entered upon lightly. The rights afforded two men who make their relationship legal are important, as are the political implications of declaring your love in front of the world. But there is something more, beyond all the politics and legalities. I will find an officiant, book that hall, call the caterers and florists, start dreaming about honeymoon spots, and write up a guest list of my loved ones only when I have found the man who is perfect for me. In short, I will get married when I meet Prince Charming.

The Gay Couple's Guide to Wedding Planning isn't going to focus on the political ramifications of your ceremony; there are plenty of experts in that field you can turn to for guidance. This book focuses on the steps you need to take to pull off the wedding of your dreams, without getting too stressed out. In many respects, the tips that 40-year-old gay men in New York

City want are not much different than the tips 28-year-old straight women in Ohio desire. Everyone wants to do their wedding correctly, in a unique way that represents their individuality, taste, and budget.

However, unlike other wedding-planning guides, this one will concentrate on the specific wedding needs of gay men. With the advent of same-sex ceremonies, gay men and lesbians are no longer being lumped together into one category. Finally, here's a gay-wedding book just for men! Other gay-wedding books try to speak to both genders, and therefore include information that's not always relevant to one gender or the other. We're delving into wedding issues that men care about. Toward that end, I've included sections such as "Straight Talk" (in which I identify the traditional way of doing things), followed by "The Man Difference" (in which I discuss the gay way). Other recurring sections include "What Every 'Mo Needs to Know," "Queeries," "Fit to Be Tied"(celebrity fitness trainer Joey Gonzalez's fitness tips), and (my favorite) "Cheap Tricks." In addition, to see you through the frenzy of wedding planning, you'll find such lighthearted fare as "The Ten Gayest Wedding Movies Evah!" and "Are You a Groomzilla?"

The Gay Couple's Guide to Wedding Planning is the perfect book for male couples who want to understand how to take the stress out of every stage of putting together a memorable ceremony and reception. Some factors are the same as for lesbian couples (like finding a justice of the peace), but much of the planning is entirely different (grooming for grooms, for example, and such questions as: Do you need two best men? Do you throw two bachelor parties or one? Can you still throw a bouquet, and who should throw it?).

It's a wonderful sign of the times that gay weddings have become so accepted that the need for a book geared just to gay men has emerged. It's my privilege to be part of the trend.

No thank-you notes are required; I'll accept the lifetime of smiles.

David Toussaint

Chapter 1: Twelve Months Ahead
MAN TO MAN

- ☐ Decide on whom to tell first, now that you're engaged
- ☐ Research legal options, if applicable
- ☐ Figure out your budget
- ☐ Determine the style and size of your wedding
- ☐ Set the date
- ☐ Unsubscribe to Match.com

GETTING STARTED: *How to Use the 12-Month Guide*

You've been dreaming about this wedding since you rewrote the ending of *Brokeback Mountain* to give those bucking broncos a happily-ever-after cowboy-themed affair. Now that it's your turn, sit down together and figure out what kind of wedding you desire. Since there are two of you, you're going to discover that a lot of your plans are of no interest to your partner, and vice versa. Something called compromise is about to play a huge part in your life, so get used to it. While it's easy to just say, "We've got 50,000 bucks — let's call the caterer and let the chips fall where they may," knowing what you want helps all the elements fall into place. It also lays the groundwork for planning the *who*, *what*, *when*, *where*, and *why*.

To make the wedding-planning process easier, we've arranged this book in 12-month-countdown fashion. This should help you keep track of what needs to be done — and to that end, we've also included a checklist at the beginning of each chapter. Obviously, some of you will have longer engagements, and some

shorter, and it's important to note that this is merely a guide; you should rearrange according to your needs. If you're a whiz at details, but just don't know a thing about registering for gifts, by all means skip ahead to that section (Chapter 5).

Don't panic if it's two months before the wedding and you realize that the flowers should have been picked out months ago — go back to that section in the book (Chapter 5), huddle (it's a football term, guys), and get it done. Most couples have trouble with some aspect of the wedding, and that's when you come together, enlist help from friends, and resolve the issue. Be prepared, too, for emergencies; if that fabulous photographer you hired went AWOL, take a deep breath and go over your options. Everything will work out. On that note, let's get this party started! It's your time to make beautiful music together.

WEDDING PROPOSITION

Keep the romantic side of yourself alive — take that big step and propose. Since your roles are less defined than they are for a man and woman, either one of you can propose to the other. If you've been planning to get married for a long time and are working out the logistics of the wedding, it's a formality to propose — but what a sweet formality to embrace. Surprise him. Take him out to dinner, to that spot where you met, or anywhere special, anytime he's not expecting it, and tell him he's the love of your life and that you want to spend the rest of your life by his side. Whether you offer him a ring, a Champagne toast, or just a sweet kiss, it'll mean the world to him to hear the words. And for you to hear "yes" back.

OVER THE RAINBOW: *What to Do Now That You're Engaged*

No matter if your engagement is brand-new or 20 years in the making, once you decide to wed, everything changes. Your nuptials are official and plans need to be made. To keep things organized, mull over these fine points before you set the wedding date. Start from the beginning, and the end will be blissfully simpler.

PEOPLE WHO NEED PEOPLE

Sit down with your partner and decide *whom* you should tell first, and *how* you want to proceed. Don't make any decisions about the wedding party, best man, or maid of honor, and don't consider calling anyone who might not be invited to the wedding. Phone Mom and Dad, if they're accepting of your relationship, and call your close friends. If there's one thing I've learned from being in this business for more than a decade, it's that guys want to call their "girlfriends" as well as their girl friends right after it's official. While that's understandable, hold on. In the meantime, take time to savor your engagement with the one you love — that guy looking over your shoulder.

MAN UP

If your relationship is out in the open, and your loved ones are accepting, telling them will be a simple, joyous occasion. If there are obstacles, tread carefully. For any relative who is unlikely to be supportive of your engagement but is going to find out about your wedding, pick a time to tell him or her, and a method. For supportive parents, take them out to lunch or dinner or invite them over. If they live far away, ask if there's a good time to speak on the phone. Don't e-mail or text. Before the wedding, do your best to make sure all parents and close relatives have met. If your parents don't know your fiancé, try to arrange a person-to-person meeting shortly after you've told them about the wedding. Even if this is an uncomfortable task, it's going to be a lot easier to introduce them now than right after you've said your vows.

TOT TALK

Keep children in mind, too. If you already have kids, they need to know about your wedding immediately. Gossip spreads, and all it takes is one loose-lipped friend for children to find out they're about to get a new dad. Plan a time to talk to children, and make it soon. Depending on how young they are, this could be a difficult situation, and you shouldn't expect them to jump for joy at the first sight of your ring. Your life is changing forever, and so is theirs. They need to know that at school they're going to be asked about their two daddies, and there might be bullying and other repercussions. If necessary, meet with a guidance counselor about how to tell your children, and certainly speak to other couples who've been down the path. There might be young family members and nieces and nephews you need to talk to as well. Each circumstance is different; when in doubt, you should be the ones to talk to them, not another relative.

HEART TO HEART:
Our Journey to the Wedding

The best thing we did was to invite friends with kids. It wasn't so many that it turned into a day-care nightmare, but it was enough that we have stories about them hiding the officiant's clothes. Today, there are eight- and nine-year-olds who tell their classmates that the first wedding they went to was for Uncles Ted and Ian. Now I'd like to take our three-year-old son to a same-sex wedding.

— TED PETERSON, MARRIED TO IAN SMITH, 2007

LAW, FIRM: *Understanding Your Legal Options*

In today's world, your wedding might be the stamp on your already-licensed marriage or a platform to signing papers. If you haven't thought much about your options, but would like some sort of legal recognition, do your research now. For marriage, check the rules for your state as well as the state your partner lives in, if it's different from your own. You also might need to investigate marriages abroad, and your state's legal recognition of an out-of-country wedding. Check into civil unions and domestic partnerships, if you haven't done so already. Since the laws for same-sex marriage vary dramatically, and almost daily, your legal options need to be understood and handled now, so that there are no 11th-hour surprises.

MONEY MAKES THE WORLD GO AROUND:
Knowing Your Budget

Money isn't always the most pleasant thing to discuss, so think of it like your leg workout and get it over with immediately. Decide how much you want to spend, how much you can spend, and how much extra you have if there are unexpected surprises (and there will be). Also find out whether or not anyone else is contributing. A good chunk of gay men pay for the wedding themselves; if that's the case, this is a shorter discussion. If Mom or Dad or your Godmother (Fairy or otherwise) is pitching in, now's the time to find out how much. You're not being greedy, just pragmatic. Many gay couples are told that one of the parents is going to pitch in, only to find out a few months later that the parent in question has changed his or her mind.

THE PARENTAL TRAP

Parents' contributions can be a touchy subject for man-to-man marriage, as sometimes even the most liberal-seeming family can change its tune when "wedding" is added

to the relationship. If Mom or Dad has doubts, don't push it. A wedding isn't the time to wage a gay-liberation war. Even if your sister's wedding was entirely paid for by Dad, he might think twice about doing the same for you and your husband. All you can do is tell him how you feel, decide how that affects his role in the wedding, and move on. You'll be much happier with a small wedding filled with people who support your union than with a big, splashy affair where half the people are snickering at your "vows."

VISION QUEST:
The Who, What, Where, When, and Why of Choosing Your Wedding Style

This is the time for making decisions. Whether you have a vision of what you've always wanted your wedding to be like or you're just beginning to consider your options, here are some pointers on choosing your wedding style.

FORMALLY YOURS

One of the decisions to be made is how formal you guys want to go. You can do the full-out black-tie event or khakis and linen. The former means you need the proper reception venue, and the latter means you should probably be thinking outdoors and warm weather. Black-tie events aren't suited for the morning, so consider time of day when thinking about the level of formality. Your budget is obviously going to play a major role in this decision, as big, fancy weddings don't come cheap. If you know your budget is small, rule out Friday night at the Plaza, and start thinking about a daytime ceremony at home and a restaurant or club reception. Formal also tends to mean "large," which leads us to the next decision.

SIZE MATTERS

Two hundred people at a wedding generally implies a formal affair, whereas 30 friends almost always translates to casual dress. You might find that the number of people you have at your event, combined with your budget, is what determines the formality of the occasion. Think of the weddings you've been to, start counting up those "must-haves," and then add your own vision. You should know, too, that many sites have a guest minimum, and that going anywhere that involves airline travel (and time off from work) for guests is going to change the guest count.

GAINING YOUR RELIGION

If you're set on a religious ceremony, you've just upped the formality level (people aren't going to wear flip-flops in church, no matter what you say on the invitation). If you've decided on a large wedding, know that some of those guests probably won't be able to fit into the house of worship. Yes, you can invite people solely to the reception, but that's a slippery slope many couples choose to avoid. A religious venue would be relatively easy to secure if the two of you were straight; your gay nuptials require extra time to find the site that welcomes you with open arms.

TIME/CLOCK OF THE HEART

While many guys are set on that starry, starry nighttime affair, others prefer Sunday in the Park with Gorgeous. In addition to your own wants, consider your guests and what they'll enjoy most. If lots of elderly people are attending, early is often good (post-parties can be fantastic). If you want to get married somewhere that has an enviable view of the sunset, consider a late-afternoon cocktail reception. There's always a time for love; pick the hour and let your heart start ticking. People often go the unconventional route, too, with everything from afternoon teas to late-night-party weddings. You're here, you're queer, do whatever you want for your wedding, and have no fear.

A SHORT TIME FROM NOW IN A GALAXY QUITE CLOSE TO HOME

Long-distance weddings are wonderful and exquisite. Know that you're going to have to hire vendors at the site (though some couples also bring their own vendors from home). Be aware that, when abroad, you might have restrictions on the cake, food, flowers, and other personal touches. Long-distance weddings also mean fewer guests, as it's difficult, and expensive, for many people to fly off to witness your vows. On the bright side, your honeymoon's already included.

SEASONS AND GREETINGS

Picking the time of year to get married can involve practicality, money, location, even the site you want — that fantastic hall might be booked until February. Your jobs might mean you have to wait until summer, and if you want that snowy ski wedding, winter calls. If you do pick a holiday weekend, or day, plan far in advance, as your guests are going to need to take time off from work and to make their own vacation plans. If that spring wedding means you have four months to prepare, consider waiting another year or switching themes — putting a "rush" order on your wedding is the easiest way to set yourself up for disappointment.

NEXT TO NORMAL?

It's important to note that while gay weddings have made great strides in the past several years, a lot of men still want a fun, fabulous, over-the-top "gay" wedding, and we applaud them. There's no rule that says you need to conform to society's definition of a wedding, so go with your heart. If that means a nude affair in your backyard, drop, er, everything and start planning. If you want a witch to bless you on the beach, jump that broom. In the world of gay weddings, all that's changed is the number of men who are comfortable enough in their skin to say "I do."

You have a good idea of how much money you can spend, you know the formality of the affair, you've told your friends and loved ones, and you've removed all porn sites from your computers. Now it's time to figure out the day you're going to have the ceremony.

First off, have alternate dates set. It's no fun to be a killjoy, but this is a must, especially if you're set on a specific site or a holiday. New Year's Eve may be impossible no matter where you want to book, and that divine cliff-top restaurant might be closed on Sundays. Even if your wedding is on the date of the anniversary when you met and it's a Thursday in October and you're planning a backyard affair, have an alternate date *just in case*. You might have everything set, only to discover you've planned your dream wedding on the same date Mom and Dad are spending their 40th anniversary in Prague.

IF WE TOOK A HOLIDAY

Festive holidays are a wonderful time to tie the knot, as are long weekends like Memorial Day or the Fourth of July. Once again, before you pick a holiday, consider how it will affect the guest list. Does your circle of friends travel a lot over that weekend? Budgetwise, will it be affordable for guests? (Travel and accommodations on holidays are almost always more expensive than at other times.) Also, Christmas and Hanukkah can be very complicated times of the year for family, so think of what adding a wedding to that festive mix can mean.

THE NEARNESS OF YOU

Go over all of the above, narrow down and cross off, take into consideration seasons and time and formality and budget and everything else discussed thus far, and pick that date for your wedding. After you take care of a few "minor" details, all you have to do is just show up!

STAYING ON TOP OF GETTING ORGANIZED

Decide how you're going to organize the events leading up to your big day, whether it's with an iPad, your PC, binders, pads of paper, or, for the real control freaks among you, renting a storage unit to hold swatches and centerpiece selections. Whatever method you choose, make sure both parties are aware of the system created, and stick with it. Delegate tasks now. Decide who's best at being the diplomat, and who's stronger with contracts and negotiations. There's a reason why wedding checklists are so popular in printed planners — you need the satisfaction and reassurance that you're getting things done in the correct order.

Remember, planning a wedding does *not* mean giving up your life. Make a concerted effort to eat right, to exercise, and to sleep. While that may sound like childish or unnecessary advice now, it won't once you're in the thick of arranging your wedding. You guys agreed to tie the knot because you love each other, and because you're always going to be there for each other. Start now. Watch over each other and be supportive through the days ahead. That's a little bit of wisdom that you can use for the rest of your lives.

CONTRACT HITS

In the next several months, you're going to be reviewing and signing a lot of contracts. Know the basics now, and you'll save yourself from a lot of hassles later on. When dealing with every vendor, you need to get, *in writing*, the amount

To help you out, we've asked celebrity fitness trainer Joey Gonzalez, Chief Operating Officer of the popular Barry's Bootcamp, to give you 12 tips, one for each month. Now put the book down, get your ass out of bed, and shape up!

MONTH 12 — You're getting married in a year, so look at yourself naked at least once in the morning. Then decide if you really need to eat that bagel. Turkey bacon and egg whites instead.
— *Joey Gonzalez*

of the deposit required (never pay the full amount of anything up front), overtime fees, cancellation fees should you decide to discontinue the vendor's services, and all the other specifics agreed upon. Never expect anything that is not written down. If a photographer offers to shoot your engagement photo as part of your package, he or she needs to put it in writing. If the florist says he'll throw in some hydrangeas, make him say it with a pen. For your own protection, you need to know the name of substitute caterers, florists, musicians, and DJs, in case of emergency. You also need to know what your refund is if any vendor makes a mistake or doesn't come through as promised. If you're ordering a limousine, make sure "black" is written down, so you don't pull up to your wedding in one of Prince's purple throwaways. Whenever you're talking to a vendor, don't assume he or she will be the one baking the cake or preparing the food or singing in the band. Specific names are e ssential, as a lot of people use assistants for weddings. Once you've signed contracts, make hard copies and keep them in a safe place. Finally, if you are unclear or uneasy about any portion of a contract, ask for it to be clarified. Only sign when you feel comfortable doing so.

Proposition Gr8

I told my boyfriend I was taking him to dinner for our one-year anniversary. After we opened presents, I slipped around the table and, on my knees, ring in hand, asked him to marry me. Of course, it being us, the ring was a toe ring I'd found at a souvenir shop, with a male figure on it, appropriately goofy for two very nerdy boys.

His response? "Really? You want to marry me?" I nodded, and he said yes. Then I took him to a hotel I'd reserved, with a pool. Inside, there was a bottle of scotch, two pairs of slippers, and two pairs of women's boxer shorts complete with hearts all over them — I'd gone to the dollar store earlier and bought the only thing remotely resembling swimsuits they had to offer. It was one of the best nights of my life.

— Randy Roberts Potts, married to Keaton Johnson, May 26, 2012

The Ten Gayest Weddings Ever

1. Liza Minnelli and David Gest (New York City, March 16, 2002)

WHY IT'S FOR HOMOS: She's a gay icon and the daughter of a legend, and he's a . . . let's just stick with her for now.

WHY IT'S A FABULOUS AFFAIR: A $3.5 million wedding with 500 guests that included Diana Ross, Lauren Bacall, Mia Farrow, and maid of honor Elizabeth Taylor. And Tony Bennett entertained. Now that's class.

WHY YOU MIGHT WANT TO RETHINK COPYING THEIR STYLE: Hopefully, your groom came out ages ago.

IMITATION OF LIFE: Hire a Liza drag queen to perform. Extra points if you get the wedding-party guys to line kick to "New York, New York."

2. Sir Elton John and David Furnish (England, December 21, 2005)

WHY IT'S FOR HOMOS: They may call him "Sir," but we all know he's the queen.

WHY IT'S A FABULOUS AFFAIR: They wed in the same place where Prince Charles and Camilla Parker Bowles tied the knot.

WHY YOU MIGHT WANT TO RETHINK COPYING THEIR STYLE: Some of your guests might take the Elton persona a bit too far and start trashing every guest at the event.

IMITATION OF LIFE: Ben & Jerry's® designed the wedding cake! Serve their yummy-licious ice cream at your affair, or call your baker and see if you can have an ice-cream cake made for your nuptials. Feel free to inscribe "The Bitches Are Back" on top.

3. Ellen DeGeneres and Portia de Rossi (California, August 16, 2008)

WHY IT'S FOR HOMOS: 'Cause we men only wish we could be as hot as these chicks.

WHY IT'S A FABULOUS AFFAIR: Los Angeles, a warm summer night and the brides wore white, close friends, an all-vegan menu, and red velvet cake. They even sat on pillows for the vows.

WHY YOU MIGHT WANT TO RETHINK COPYING THEIR STYLE: You'll never stop fighting over who gets to wear the dress.

IMITATION OF LIFE: Vegan menus are all the rage; ditto organic affairs. And marrying at home is gay chic.

4. Barbra Streisand and James Brolin (California, July 1, 1998)

WHY IT'S FOR HOMOS: She's the Queen of Everything and he's the Hottest Senior Citizen Alive.

WHY IT'S A FABULOUS AFFAIR: They wed at her Malibu home (with 4,000 roses) exactly two years after their first date. The bride wore Donna Karan, natch. And Sadie, Sadie sang to her hubby.

WHY YOU MIGHT WANT TO RETHINK COPYING THEIR STYLE: And you think *you're* a perfectionist? Try organizing an entire affair while only showing the left side of your face.

IMITATION OF LIFE: A Streisand marathon is a must, starting with *Funny Girl* and ending with *What's Up, Doc?* Your drag-queen friends will keep you up all night with their "like buttah" impersonations.

5. Belle and the Beast, *Beauty and the Beast* (France, Once Upon a Time . . .)

WHY IT'S FOR HOMOS: One's a beauty, the other's an irresistible beast. Or, as your friends like to call you, the Twink and the Bear.

WHY IT'S A FABULOUS AFFAIR: A Technicolor castle and singing teapots. It's the closest thing you'll get to those Ecstasy days.

WHY YOU MIGHT WANT TO RETHINK COPYING THEIR STYLE: Have you done an online search? *Beauty and the Beast*–themed weddings are more popular than a top in Fort Lauderdale.

IMITATION OF LIFE: Four words: Gay Days Disney honeymoon!

6. Elizabeth Taylor and Conrad Hilton, Michael Wilding, Michael Todd, Eddie Fisher, Richard Burton (twice), John Warner, Larry Fortensky (1950 to 1991)

WHY IT'S FOR HOMOS: She loved gay men almost as much as you do.

WHY IT'S A FABULOUS AFFAIR: It's Liz we're talking about — pigs in a blanket would be fabulous with Taylor in tow.

WHY YOU MIGHT WANT TO RETHINK COPYING THEIR STYLE: You do know she had eight weddings, right?

IMITATION OF LIFE: Have an Elizabeth Taylor marriage–themed party, and make the guests go as their favorite Taylor wedding look. Winner gets a diamond, or White Diamonds.

7. Madonna and Sean Penn (California, August 16, 1986)

WHY IT'S FOR HOMOS: She's the Material Girl and he's the Bad Boy.

WHY IT'S A FABULOUS AFFAIR: Held on a Malibu cliff top (on M's birthday, no less), the vows were drowned out by paparazzi helicopters hovering above. And Cher and Andy Warhol attended.

WHY YOU MIGHT WANT TO RETHINK COPYING THEIR STYLE: She nixed all of her own music for the reception, and he nixed anyone's face who got close to his wife.

IMITATION OF LIFE: Have a "Dress Up as Your Favorite Madonna Incarnation" prenuptial party. It'll be the most MDN-GAY bash of the year.

8. Celine Dion and René Angélil (Quebec, December 17, 1994)

WHY IT'S FOR HOMOS: Did you see her headdress? A drag queen couldn't pull that one off — or a crane.

WHY IT'S A FABULOUS AFFAIR: A 21-string orchestra, led by David Foster at the piano, greeted the guests.

WHY YOU MIGHT WANT TO RETHINK COPYING THEIR STYLE: Their cake looked like a Christmas tree that had thrown up — on the bride's dress.

IMITATION OF LIFE: Have a prewedding Vegas bash with Dion tickets, natch. Or just see one of the many wickedly good impersonators of her in the drag shows.

9. Princess Diana and Prince Charles (England, July 29, 1981)

WHY IT'S FOR HOMOS: She married a prince. Unless you skipped fairy tales 101, that's every gay child's dream come true.

WHY IT'S A FABULOUS AFFAIR: They wed at St. Paul's Cathedral (there was more seating than at less-posh Westminster Abbey), her ring consisted of 14 diamonds surrounding a sapphire, and her dress had a 25-foot train. Oh, yeah, and 75 million people watched it on TV.

WHY YOU MIGHT WANT TO RETHINK IMITATING THEIR STYLE: Seriously?

IMITATION OF LIFE: Eat a lot of apples, and have your own prince wake you up with a gorgeous kiss. And if that doesn't float your boat, head to England and crown yourselves Queens for a Day.

10. Kevin Keller and Clay Walker (Riverdale, January 5, 2012)

WHY IT'S FOR HOMOS: They're comic book characters in *Life with Archie*, and colored-in saints.

WHY IT'S A FABULOUS AFFAIR: Kevin, an Iraq War vet, met his hot doctor while recuperating in the hospital. And who wouldn't want Veronica to help celebrate your nuptials!

WHY YOU MIGHT WANT TO RETHINK COPYING THEIR STYLE: Cartoon cocktails suck.

IMITATION OF LIFE: Not unlike a lot of gay couples, the lovers faced a few haters (in this case, A Million Moms, who demanded that Toys "R" Us® remove the offending issue off the racks). Despite the few protesters against love, the comic sold out of stores. Yep, that's the future of gay weddings!

Chapter 2: Eleven Months Ahead
FAMILY AFFAIR

- [ ] Create a budget breakdown of where your money will be allocated
- [ ] Choose your wedding party
- [ ] Decide on a preliminary guest list
- [ ] Book the ceremony site, reception site, and caterer
- [ ] Meet with your officiant
- [ ] Send out save-the-date cards
- [ ] Cross off "dating" from your to-do list and move it to your done-to-death list

WHAT GOES WHERE: *A Budget Breakdown*

In Chapter 1, we told you to figure out how much money you can afford to spend on your wedding, and to start planning with that figure in mind. Now that you're in the second month, it's good to have an idea of *where* that cash is headed. Knowing the price of cake isn't just a piece of delicious trivia; like many couples, and especially many gay couples, you might find that there are expenses you want to cut back on, or delete altogether, and other ones you'd like to buff up. Here's a brief summary of traditional wedding expenses:

50 percent: Reception. Yes, approximately 50 percent of your money is going to that reception, which includes the site, the food, the drink, and all that other jazz.

10 percent: Photography. If this makes you wince, take a look in the mirror. Yep, you're already on your way to doubling this number.

5 percent each: Flowers, attire, music: total of 15 percent. The good news? You're men, so there might not be an expensive wedding gown involved. The bad news? You're gay men, so you'll find a way to spend that money elsewhere.

25 percent: Everything else. Keep in mind that this figure includes your honeymoon, assuming that's in your plans. Know, too, that before you decide you're already ahead of the game, everything costs more than you think. There's an old budget saying that goes "Stick to a budget, then double it." Hopefully, it won't come to that, but always expect to spend more than you've allotted.

STRAIGHT TALK

Once upon a time, when a couple fell in love, the bride's parents paid for the wedding, the groom's parents paid for the rehearsal dinner and the flowers, and the groom paid for (and picked) the honeymoon and his fiancée's beautiful ring.

THE MAN DIFFERENCE

Times change, and so do budget breakdowns. Gay couples are rethinking every aspect of their weddings, from the cake to the bachelor party. Decide where you want to scale back and where you want to splurge. If a rehearsal dinner is not a priority, make it a lunch or breakfast, or nix it altogether (but not the rehearsal). As you start contacting vendors and getting ideas, you'll find some areas that are extremely important (maybe that three-course meal), and some that are not (if you're not wearing a Vera Wang gown or buying a diamond ring, you just saved a bundle). Most important, if there is one area that you both have your hearts set on, find a way to make it happen and then agree to cut something else.

THE BOYS (AND GIRLS) IN THE BAND: *Choosing Your Wedding Party*

You've had a month to get somewhat grounded, which means now's the best time to determine whom you want in your wedding. Since you've figured out the approximate size and style of your wedding, as well as the budget, your job of picking party dudes should be a bit simpler. And before you decide that your anal-attentive, control-freak nature means you need to do everything yourself, and that any "attendant" is only going to screw things up, remember the stress you're about to endure, as well as the comfort — and fun — wedding-party members provide. Read the following if you're clueless about all the things attendants are responsible for doing.

STRAIGHT TALK: Best Man, Maid of Honor

Traditionally, the best man (or, if you wish, a maid or matron of honor) is your right-hand guy. He helps pick out the tux, arranges the bachelor party, and takes care of emergencies as they crop up. He's responsible for getting the tuxes back to the shop, providing the rings, and holding cash that's needed at the wedding (tips for taxis, money for the officiant, etc.). He's also the personal babysitter for you and your other half, making sure the two of you make that flight to Palm Springs.

GROOMSMEN AND BRIDESMAIDS

Groomsmen and bridesmaids (and guess what? You can have both!) help with all parties, attend all wedding-related events, wear wedding outfits, and generally make you look even hotter than you already are. You can have 20 or you can have three — it all depends on the kind of wedding you want, and budget restrictions. As for outfits, the look for men is generally a variation on the grooms' attire. If you're going for a mix-and-match ensemble, you might consider having the guys pick their own look, with guidelines to keep it close to your theme. Should there be a bachelor party or shower, they're expected to pitch in on the costs. Anyone can host a shindig, too, so if a member of your party wants to take this job from the best man or maid of honor, by all means let them give it a go.

USHERS

Your groomsmen serve as ushers, helping seat people and making sure everyone has a program. If you're in a house of worship, they'll need to know ahead of time about persons of interest (parents, etc.), so they can seat them in the right place. If you have a receiving line, it's smart to put an usher in charge of herding the crowd to the front of the building. As for walking down the aisle, this is a *gay* wedding, folks. No one's going to blink if the ushers walk down the aisle together. If there are women, you can go traditional, and have the men escort them.

THE MAN DIFFERENCE

Having a female friend take over as the best man is easier for gay men than straight men. For one thing, you probably already have a lot of gal pals who'd *love* to do the job. A woman isn't going to flinch when you talk about strippers or sexy underwear; quite the opposite. Since women tend to have more wedding experience than men (in practice, anyway), they can be a welcome relief when hassles arise. Also, should you go the bachelor-party route, complete with strippers or anything else salacious, your girlfriend will probably have as much fun planning the event as you will have attending it. You can call her a maid of honor or matron of honor, or best woman, if she prefers. Or, you can skip those names altogether and just refer to her as an attendant or your confidante, or any other title you like. If there are other women in the wedding party, the best woman's outfit should complement their look. If there are only men present, or if she wants to dress like one of the boys, by all means let her choose her own look or take on one of theirs.

THE KIDS ARE ALL RIGHT

Children can be flower girls, ring bearers, junior bridesmaids, or ushers. There is no obligation to include children in your wedding, and some people feel it's too hard on the kids and a nuisance for everyone else. Know that if you're going to have children involved in your wedding, many guests will assume their children are invited. Allowing children at your wedding is your choice to make, and if you decide on an "adults only" ceremony, some people are likely to break the rule and show up with kids in tow, or call and ask if it's okay if Little Louise and Dainty June come along. Be polite but firm in your negative response. You can also be a great help to guests by finding babysitters in the area and including that information on your Web site, via e-mail, or in reception details. If your friend Mike Meme does show up with his six-year-old tyke, grin and bear it.

CHILD'S PLAY

If there are children at the wedding, consider arranging activities for them, separate tables, and a different menu. You can hire entertainment and an on-site sitter. Children get tired easily, especially when they're dressed up and told to be quiet, so the more distractions they have to occupy themselves, the better for all involved. If the children are all staying at the same hotel, consider hiring a sitter who'll accompany them back there once the party starts getting late, and who'll remain with them at the hotel.

BODY COUNT: *Creating Your Guest List*

And you thought the front row at a Madonna concert was chaos. Creating your guest list is usually one of engaged couples' biggest headaches, so prepare yourself. While you don't need to work on your guest list yet (those invitations won't be sent out until about two months prior to your wedding), it's a task that's best started immediately. Think of your guest list like preparing taxes: it's not due until April 15th, but the sooner you start getting all the information together, the less of a hassle you'll have when the crunch arrives.

STRAIGHT TALK

Traditionally, the first thing you need to do is take into account how much money parents are contributing. If it's a good chunk of cash, they should have a say as to who's invited. This doesn't mean they're in charge of the list, but you want to do the best to honor their wishes. Once you go through their requests, the time-honored tradition is to split the list up 50-50, with the bride's friends and family on one side of the ceremony spot, and the groom's on the other.

THE MAN DIFFERENCE

In the gay world, your parents might not be contributing any money for your wedding — and, sadly, one or more of them might not even approve. Gay men tend to marry later in life than straight couples, with two incomes to help pay for the wedding. If there are no outside contributions, the guest list is all yours — though do consider friendly family requests.

DOUBLE YOUR PLEASURE

As for splitting up the guest list, go for it if it's the easiest way to solve any disputes. Depending on your social circles and how long you've been together, it might be easier and more fun to pick the invites as a team. Start with your relatives and closest friends, then branch out. Even if you're planning an intimate ceremony at a restaurant, or a quiet Key West brunch, as soon as you start putting down names, more names will pop up in your head. Hurt feelings are best kept at a minimum, so a common rule of thumb is to start with a set amount of people, then plan to double the list.

YOU GOTTA WORK

Officemates can be tricky, and the traditional invitation guidelines are best: invite no coworkers, just your boss, or invite everyone in your department. Don't leave out the graphic designer who sits next to you because he was for Hillary and you campaigned for Obama; politics are ugly pretty much all the time and you don't want to infuse them into your wedding. If you aren't completely out at work, or know that many of your officemates are homophobic, your best bet is to leave the clan off the list. Hey, you'll save some money, too.

THE SECOND COMING

No matter how big your wedding, and how unlimited your budget, you're not going to be able to invite everyone you'd like. Your B-list of guests is imperative, because if you've planned for 100 guests, some of them will RSVP "no." Unlike that Logo TV series, in the real world an A-list actually has substance. Once you go through the must-haves, move on to the second category. When the "no's" start coming back from your first group, send out invitations to the second one. Before you send out the second round of invitations, make sure the nonresponders aren't just being lazy. Call or e-mail them to find out if they plan on attending. If someone backs out at the last minute, and you have an open spot, it's okay to call and invite a friend.

Many people worry that guests will be offended if they know they weren't invited right off the bat. There is no need to explain to any friend or relative why they didn't get an invitation the same week as your sister, Susan; this is *your* wedding, and these are *your* decisions. If someone confronts you about the issue (and they shouldn't), politely tell them the truth — that it was impossible to put everyone on the guest list from day one.

GET THIS PARTY STARTED:
Book the Ceremony Site, Reception Venue, and Caterer

That deep breath you just took was a great way to gear up for the serious fun ahead. Booking your ceremony site and/or your reception venue, as well as your caterer, takes a lot of hard work. Done right, it's more thrilling than Barbra going off her teleprompter. While it may seem overwhelming at first, it gets much easier as you start putting all the elements together. Take it nice and slow, relax, and know that in the end it's going to be amazing. Kind of like your wedding night!

BOOKING THE CEREMONY SITE

You know when you want to have your wedding, you know your budget, you know the style and formality of your affair, and you know how many guests you'd like in attendance. Having those decisions behind you makes booking your site a thousand times easier. If you already have a place in mind, call now and find out if it's available. Ask about alternate dates and times. If they have a reasonable waiting list, take advantage of the option. However, don't allow the wait to drag on, and don't assume they'll find room for you. Start looking elsewhere.

CHURCH CHAT

If you're already planning a ceremony in a house of worship, you probably have a good idea of where the affair will be held. If not, talk to the officiant to narrow down your search. Before you book, go over the details to make sure the spot has everything you need. For a house of worship, it's imperative that there is adequate parking, bathrooms,

Queeries

When booking any site, some questions can't go unanswered.
Read on for tips.

Q. Are there any clothing requirements or other restrictions for your site?

A. You might find that the church of choice doesn't allow musicians inside (there goes the violinist). Ditto some of the more conservative restaurants or venues. They also might not allow indoor photography in every area, or even sleeveless dresses. Go through all your questions with the person in charge. Never assume anything.

Q. What is included in the space?

A. You walk into a gorgeous venue and book it on the spot. Only later do you find that all the décor was rented for a previous wedding. Find out what the site offers (including tables, chairs, and plants), and what you need to rent or have the caterer provide.

Q. What can I add?

A. On the flip side, if you love a site but hate the tables, are you allowed to provide your own? How much "decorating" will a site permit? Most houses of worship are pretty strict about allowing anything to be brought in, so make sure you discuss every "innovation." Rice throwing isn't only out of style because it's bad for birds; a lot of venues don't want to deal with cleaning up the mess. They also might not want to pick up those adorable rose petals scattered all over the floor.

Q. How do we stay dry?

A. If your ceremony is outside, at a beach, park, garden, or outdoor restaurant, have a Plan B. I don't care how seldom it rains in Dry Rot, Arizona, or what the weather forecast says for the next six months — a rain plan is a must. You should have one for the ceremony site, and one for the reception site as well. The good news is that most outdoor spots have already figured this out. It's up to you to follow through and find out exactly where the alternate vows or reception will take place. Make sure you inspect the second site to confirm it's up to snuff. Also, discuss any additional fees that a rain plan might include.

changing rooms, and, most important, enough seats inside to fit your guest list. Churches and synagogues often schedule events close together, so you need to make sure that another event isn't being held 20 minutes after yours is scheduled to end.

PLACES, PLEASE

If you're not sure where you want the affair, start narrowing down your choices. Your best bet for ideas comes from friends' suggestions and their own wedding spots, vendors, and personal experiences. If you love that Malibu beach restaurant, find out if it holds weddings. Parks and beaches are fantastic, but they come with rules. (You may not be able to serve liquor.) If you're set on a fancy soirée in a ritzy hotel, but are worried it might not be gay friendly, check out the IGLTA (International Gay & Lesbian Travel Association), which lists its members all over the world. Take time to go over those favorite spots of yours — where you had your first date, where you first said, "I love you," the hotel where Kylie stayed when in town — and start calling.

STRAIGHT TALK

Traditional weddings, more often than not, are held in a house of worship, with the reception to follow at a popular wedding venue. Like, ahem, "traditional marriage," this is how it's been done forever, and there's nothing wrong with that. The downside to popular reception sites is that they can result in cookie-cutter weddings that look like every other affair you've attended. You might want to think twice before booking that venue where those popular steadies Brenda and Eddie got hitched.

THE MAN DIFFERENCE

You're making up the rules, so break them. Like gay marriage, gay weddings are changing the way ceremonies are being held. Couples are rethinking what's inside the box, and rethinking the site. Houses of worships are often nixed because of homophobic connotations, and guys are going all elegant. They're also going a bit crazy, hiring event planners as gay as Liza Minnelli's scarf, with ice bars and French Revolution themes and after parties that look like something out of Studio 54's glory days. Restaurants are big news, as are private clubs and boutique hotels. Do whatever you like, but keep an open mind. You might find that traditional spots are as outdated as the vow "till death do us part."

SETTING A GOOD EXAMPLE

Gay weddings are big business these days, and that's wonderful. However, never try to get something for free or at a reduced rate because of your "minority status." Vendors need to work too, and they need to make money. The only haggling you should ever do is of the practical kind: reducing the hours, limiting the bar, picking a Tuesday evening. We're relatively new to the wedding picture, so let's try to set a good example for future generations.

BOOKING THE RECEPTION VENUE

For advice on alternate dates and times, see "Booking the Ceremony Site" (page 33). The reception venue, if different from where you'll be saying your vows, is probably one of the most exciting wedding-planning steps you'll face. Chances are you've dreamed of this spot and imagined partying on the premises till dawn. If you know the place you want, book it now. If you're undecided or clueless, talk to friends and vendors, and think of all the wonderful parties you've attended and where they were held. Don't rule out museums, sculpture gardens, or any other "nontraditional" site.

If you do have a particular place in mind, talk to the staff about availability and options. Tell them ASAP the kind of budget you're working with, and see if they can work their magic at your price. Should you be looking into a favorite restaurant or club, chances are the caterer will be on-site. Find out if you're allowed to provide outside services (and, if so, how many?). You also need to go over essentials like where the band and/or DJ will set up, where the dance floor will be (and if you need to have a floor installed), and where you'll hold the cocktail hour.

Queeries

Just as with the ceremony spot, there are essential questions
that you need to ask when booking a reception venue.
Here are some of the most important points to resolve.

Q. What do you provide, and what do I need to supply?

A. Every reception spot is different, and you might book a place that demands you use everything on-site, from the caterer to the cake, the chairs and table, and the dishes. On the flip side, never assume anything you see is up for grabs. After you survey the site, find out specifically what is yours for the wedding. Make sure every piece of décor and service is listed on the contract.

Q. What's the kitchen setup?

A. Some areas don't have kitchens at all, which means your caterer will have to bring in his or her own supplies or cook the food off-premises. If you're not using an on-site caterer, find out how well equipped the kitchen is, as well as the availability of storage areas. (That cake's gotta be placed somewhere before it's brought out!) Details need to be addressed immediately. If there are any kitchen items the site lacks, see if you can let the caterer use yours. For example, you might save a lot of money by bringing in your own blender.

Q. What are the overtime fees?

A. Many reception sites are a blast and a half until 10 p.m., when the lights come up and you have to leave — before you've even had a chance to cut the cake. Book the site for enough hours, and discuss overtime fees (assuming they offer extra hours). Some bars might go "public" after a certain hour, which means the locals might be "crashing" your wedding. If you're in an exclusive site, the "end hour" might be nonnegotiable; all of that needs to be spelled out in the contract.

Q. Is there enough parking and handicapped access?

A. Find out the parking situation, and whether or not the site provides the valet service or if you are expected to hire someone. Make sure the site has handicapped entrances and exits; this is especially important if you have lots of elderly people attending the wedding.

Q. What restrictions does the site have?

A. Find out if there's a dress code, and inquire about seemingly minute issues like whether or not red wine can be served. (Some sites frown on it.) The site might not allow loud bands, due to its proximity to neighbors, and it might not allow children or pets. Get all of your questions out of the way now.

WHERE NOT TO CUT BACK

Everyone wants to save money, but you don't want to sacrifice tact or elegance. Here are a couple of money-saving no-no's. Remember, if there's one thing worse than a cheap queen, it's the vicious queens who will talk about your wedding for years to come.

Cash Bar. Just say no. Would you invite friends over for dinner and then charge them for the wine? A cash bar is tackier than Snooki in Spandex®, and something that should always be avoided. If you can't afford the liquor, delete it from the reception — simple as that.

Tips and Tolls. Guests should never be expected to tip anyone, including bartenders, coat-check people, and valets. Take care of all gratuities yourself, and make sure everyone you hire knows they are not allowed to accept tips from guests — reliable vendors will already know this.

Ad Men. Advertising is for the media, not your wedding. While it might sound great when Hot Boy Liquors offers to give you free Stoli® in exchange for a plug, it's not going to look so terrific when your family table has a "Hot Boy" placard attached. Once again, cut back elsewhere. This one will haunt you longer than a deer tick from Fire Island.

Bad Wrap. Sure, plastic glasses and plates don't break, but they're "tray" gauche. Ditto the plastic silverware and everything else that you'd normally recycle after a day on the beach. Spend the extra dough on the real stuff — it's surprisingly less expensive to rent than you think.

Could Go Either Way. Favors are fun and kind of fabulous, but they're also expensive and not a wedding requirement. Traditional etiquette doesn't demand favors, so you're not breaking any rules if you nix the matches (who smokes anymore?) and the picture frames (who frames pictures anymore?). On the other hand, everyone likes a reminder of your wedding, and favors serve that purpose. Ultimately, if you need to cut back on the reception budget, this is an easy place to start.

BOOKING THE CATERER

When booking the caterer, you finally have the chance to create your dream menu, whether it's roast duck or fried clams and French fries. Dream big even if your budget is small. Once the two of you have narrowed down your food choices, start your search. Ask friends, relatives, and vendors for suggestions, and sift through your memories of fabulous dinners of yore. If you've got a favorite restaurant, find out if it'll cater. If it doesn't, ask the staff for recommendations. Ditto dessert chefs. Once you narrow your search, make sure you get referrals, and ask the caterer to send a couple of sample menus to see if you're on the same menu page. Don't give in when the first caterer tells you that vegan dishes are an impossibility. Do hang up and call the next caterer on your list.

Should you have any doubts about the homo-friendliness of the caterers you're interviewing, ask for gay referrals. A wedding is a wedding is a wedding, and one of the first things you need to realize on your search for vendors is that anyone who hesitates upon hearing the phrase "same-sex wedding" is a vendor you don't want to work with. No matter how good Joe's Tea Party's deviled eggs are, the staff will be "guests" at your wedding. You don't want to have any homophobes present, even if they are working behind the scenes.

$ $

CHEAP TRICKS

Here are some classic ways to save money and still pull off an amazing affair.

LIQUOR LESS. Everyone knows that booze is expensive. What you might not know is that top-shelf liquor is not required for your wedding. You can go for Smirnoff® instead of Stoli®, and no one's going to complain; if they do, pour them another drink. Also, you can skip the hard stuff altogether and serve wine and beer and a Champagne toast. These days, you can also serve sparkling wine, some of which is just as tasty as the French stuff. Or, close the bar after the cocktail hour, then reopen for the cake cutting. If your guests are not big drinkers, ask the caterer or bartenders if they will charge by the liquor consumed instead of by the hour. You should also look into purchasing the alcohol yourself. A signature drink works wonders (less ingredients to purchase, and, should it be frozen, a huge "chunk" of the stuff is ice), so do think about the Matt and Marvin Mary Margarita. White wine is generally less expensive than red, and it's common for caterers to push lots of white at the beginning of the party, then move on to the reds.

THE DRY LOOK. Dry weddings are common and perfectly acceptable. The only caveat: tell your guests ahead of time so they don't expect a buzz. Dry weddings work best for morning or noon affairs. (Many of your guests might be thankful they've finally gone to a wedding that doesn't involve a two-day hangover afterward.) And, of course, you're gonna save big bucks — unless you get your coffee from Starbucks®. The other huge advantage of a dry wedding is that everyone, including yourself, will have clear, vivid memories of the affair.

THE DAYS AND TIMES OF OUR LIVES. If you don't know yet that Saturday night is the most expensive, and popular, time to hold your wedding, you're about to learn (Friday night tends to be slightly less expensive). Not only do sites book up way in advance, the bill will be significantly higher than, say, a Wednesday brunch at the same place. Daytime affairs are always cheaper, so, if cost is an issue, keep this in mind. The other advantage of a weeknight or daytime wedding? Guests don't drink as much. The downside? Unless it's on a weekend, some guests won't be able to take the time off from work, and others might have to leave early — jobs are calling.

OFF-SEASONS OF LOVE. February is cold, miserable, rainy or snowy — and that means fewer weddings! Look into the less-popular wedding months (which will vary depending on where you live), and you'll save on the site fees. You'll also have a much better chance of

booking your dream palace. Another possible advantage? Some of your friends might be thrilled that they don't have yet *another* summer wedding to attend.

THE "GUEST"IMATE. It's simple math, guys. You want to save money? Invite fewer people.

CASH, NOT COWS. There are three things guests will expect at your wedding: something to drink, something to eat — and you guys. However, you don't need to have a three-course seated meal, and you don't need to serve filet mignon. Buffets are (usually) cheaper than seated meals, and dessert can be skipped; you already have the cake. Cocktail receptions can save you a lot of money, foodwise, as can brunch or breakfast affairs.

DOUBLE VISION. Having your ceremony and reception at the same location is not only convenient for scatterbrained guests (and anyone who's going to have a difficult time with transportation), it's also a heck of a lot cheaper than paying for two spots. Even if your wedding is at your home, you can go the indoor/outdoor route. You're not going to have to worry about extra taxis or limos, maps, or — a big one — getting caught in a traffic jam and being late for your own reception.

THE VERY ROUND TABLE. Bigger tables don't just mean heartier conversations: you'll also save on centerpieces and (probably) the amount of waiters needed. Now there's something to get the guests mingling.

FOOD, INC.

The duties of a caterer vary greatly depending on the type of wedding you're planning and the site. Should you book a hall known for weddings, chances are the caterering services are included, which means *their* staff, *their* menu, and *their* cake. Some sites might give you an option on one or all of the above, whereas other sites might not offer catering services. Your caterer might be one person or an entire company, and they might provide all tables and chairs or none. They might do all the prep work and cleanup, or they might just show up and plop the food down. Some caterers include bartender services, but don't assume that's part of the arrangement. If that seems like too much information to digest, keep in mind that an excellent, professional catering company will bring up all these options and choices before *you* start asking questions.

$$

CHEAP TRICK

Have your cake sliced up, boxed, and given to guests on the way out — it's a sweet, and classy, way to save money.

STAFF AFFECTIONS

Whether the catering company consists of two people or a *Titanic*-size crew, these people are going to be a huge part of your wedding day, from start to finish. It's imperative that their style of service suits you (and that none of the servers tries to get you enrolled in gay-reparative therapy!). When interviewing catering companies, ask about the servers, especially in regard to a gay wedding. Not to sound too clichéd, but lots of catering dudes are gay, so you're probably not going to have a hard time finding gay-friendly lads and ladies. If you live in a part of the country that isn't as gay accepting (Alabama, the Upper East Side), it's essential you get references from other gay couples who've used the company. Flirty is nice, too, and know that some caterers are more hands-on, while some blend into the background. You also need to go over the uniforms of servers, and make sure they can fit into your wedding theme. True control freaks handpick all servers and bartenders.

HEAVEN KNOWS: *Meet with the Officiant*

Yep, homosexuality and religion *can* mix, and if you want to incorporate your beliefs into the ceremony, now's the time to find the appropriate officiant. If neither you nor your other half is religious, or if you simply don't want to include religion in your wedding, hold off on this step now and find a justice of the peace, judge, county clerk, or nondenominational minister at a later date.

If the two of you share the same faith, and you're comfortable speaking to an official at your house of

PROPOSITION GR8

I don't know that I'd call it a proposal, so much, but we were on a trip to Paris. I'd never been, but my boyfriend had been there a billion times. He was playing tour guide and took me to an amazingly expensive restaurant somewhere. We got turned away, even though we had reservations. My boyfriend was crushed and I was furious, and it was raining. Since we were in suits and ties, I said, "Let's go to the Ritz for drinks." We went, were drinking martinis, bitching about the evening, and I suddenly realized he was telling me we should get married when we got home. I wasn't expecting it, and it turned out to be the most beautiful night ever!

— JOE WANST, MARRIED TO PATRICK DORPHIN,
NEW YORK CITY, 2009

Q&A

QUEERIES

Here are some of the must-ask questions for the
catering companies you're considering hiring.

Q. How much food variety do they offer?

A. These days it isn't only the nonsmokers who have special needs. Vegetarian dishes are a must at weddings, and you might have a lot of vegans attending. You don't need to accommodate every request, but go over all the food options offered. Good caterers are flexible and can improvise quickly.

Q. When's the deadline for changes and requests?

A. Your guest list will change during the course of wedding planning, and you have to know when the caterer needs the full guest count and the complete menu.

Q. Can you purchase your own liquor?

A. If buying your own liquor is an option, you can save a lot of money. The unopened bottles can be returned. Before you go this route, find out if the caterer charges a corkage fee (the price for each bottle of booze opened), and make sure it's worth the price difference. Buying liquor does take time and effort, as well as a trusted friend to return the unused bottles. Keep in mind that expensive wines can actually cost more than liquor (four or five glasses per bottle versus about 20), so don't go crazy on the absolutely, fabulously expensive Merlots.

worship, approach him or her. Even if they can't or won't marry you, they should be able to point you in the right direction (it's considered unethical to bypass your own congregation and look elsewhere without first consulting your clergy). However, if your congregation is antigay, or if you do not attend a house of worship but still want a minister to officiate, you'll have to do some research. Look into meeting with a nondenominational minister who can add religious touches to your ceremony and can usually marry you outside a house of worship. The Unitarian Universalist Association is a great place to start, and you can also go online and look for religious leaders who perform same-sex marriages. Most important, ask your friends who've been married or who have ties to gay-friendly churches and officiants.

Something to consider for any couple with mixed faiths or mixed feelings about religion: two ceremonies. You can satisfy God and your mom by having a religious-themed, quiet wedding with close friends in attendance, and then have a bigger, secular bash later on. Duo affairs can be a great way to make everyone happy, and they

give you another reason to celebrate. If two officiants are involved with your wedding, and there's a marriage license, you might have to toss a coin as to which religion gets the upper hand — only one officiant can sign. Know, too, that some clergy won't marry you unless one of you converts.

IT'S NOT JUST FOR STRAIGHT PEOPLE ANYMORE

Most officiants will expect you to engage in premarital counseling. Don't shrug this off, especially if you're both 22 and met at the White Party in Palm Springs. On the other hand, if you've been together 50 years, you're probably doing something right.

Counseling is a great way for you to learn about dealing with conflict and how to compromise, as well as addressing issues you might not have given enough thought to. If you haven't figured it out yet, or learned nothing from Kim Kardashian and Britney Spears and every Bachelor, all great marriages take work.

THE TIME OF THE SEASON: *Save-the-Date Cards*

Save-the-date cards are not imperative for all weddings, and they can add up to an unnecessary expense and a waste of time and paper.

Do send them if you want your wedding over a holiday weekend, or if you're planning a long-distance event. Should your ceremony take place over Memorial Day weekend, for example, guests need to know far in advance. If you're having an extravagant wedding in Paris, your loved ones will want to make their plans as soon as possible.

TIK TOK

While some people think you should send out save-the-date cards around the six-month mark, I think it's best to inform guests of your plans as soon as you can. Look at it this way: if you were invited to a three-day wedding in Greece over the Thanksgiving holiday, how soon would you want to be informed? Obviously, before you send out save-the-date cards, you have to have the site confirmed and the preliminary guest list completed.

Also, know all the names of people being invited. Unless you plan to write "plus one" on the invites (and does anyone *really* do that?), get the exact names of guests. Guys, this one's going to be more difficult for you than for your hetero counterparts,

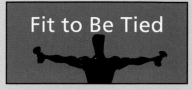

Fit to Be Tied

MONTH 11 — Think of it like this: sweat is your fat crying. Let it all out and you'll feel (and look!) much better.

— Joey Gonzalez

because a lot of your male friends probably live together and have separate names. Never invite "John Chelsea and That Guy You've Been Dating." For your friends who live with their partners, married or otherwise, each person who's invited should be listed on the card — this will be the same for the invitations — so find out everyone's correct name and spelling. Should they live apart, both guys and gals get separate invitations.

TOO CLOSE FOR COMFORT?

Another etiquette rule that can't be stressed enough: if two people are married or live together, you invite *both* of them, even if you've never met the live-in, and even if you detest him. Both of their names will be on the save-the-date card, as well as the invitation. You're not required to invite your friend or family member's lover if they're not living together, but that's an area that requires careful consideration. It might be

awkward if 90 percent of your guests bring a companion because they're married or living together, and 10 percent have to show up alone because they haven't found Mr. Right or just don't care to live with him.

YOU'VE GOT SNAIL MAIL

Save-the-date cards should be actual cards. Do not send out an e-mail and don't phone or text. Weddings are an aspect of life where some traditions never fade, and that's a plus.

Your stationer can include save-the-date cards in a package deal, or you can order them separately. There will be times later on when it's acceptable to call people or e-mail, but at this stage the pen is mightier than the smartphone. Also, make sure you send cards to everyone, even if they already know the date and location of the wedding.

HEART TO HEART:
Our Journey to the Wedding

We made clear what we expected of guests: clothing, presents, whatever. They're happy to do what you want so long as you are up-front. Nothing is more frustrating than having guests who come wearing the wrong clothes or with a present you really don't want.

— TOM VAN DEN NIEUWENHUIJZEN, MARRIED TO
PAUL VAN DEN NIEUWENHUIJZEN, THE NETHERLANDS, 2008

Chapter 3: Ten Months Ahead
READY FOR YOUR CLOSE-UP?

- [ ] Interview and book your photographer and videographer
- [ ] Take a portrait for the newspaper
- [ ] Select all stationery
- [ ] Create a wedding Web site
- [ ] Change your names, if that's your preference
- [ ] Retake your portrait for the newspaper
- [ ] Think about whether you need to hire a wedding planner
- [ ] Accept the fact that you are imperfect, and submit one of 17,000 "acceptable" shots to the newspaper

You've come a long way, baby boys. You're ten months closer to the wedding, and everything's fitting into place. This means even you anal Annies can relax — there'll be plenty of time to stress as the day approaches. Now's the time for you to start focusing on specifics and to think more about the smaller details. And before you throw yourself headfirst into the next stage, take time to see a movie, get together with friends (do *not* talk about the wedding), and keep your wits about you. It's all good.

ZOOMING IN: *Book the Photographer and Videographer*

Look at any couple's photos and videos of their wedding if you need to be reminded of the importance of photography and videography. Ask any couple what they regret about their wedding, and there's a big chance they'll say, "We should have taken more pictures." The record of your wedding is something that doesn't just last for a week after the vows; it's something you look at for the rest of your lives. Take your time seeking the right persons for these jobs, and don't make any rash decisions. Ask family and friends and other vendors, and search for gay-friendly photographers in your area.

No matter how tempting it is, and no matter what your budget, don't skimp on these two areas. Also, do not hire a fabulous photographer or videographer who's never shot a wedding, even if he or she offers you an amazing discount. Shooting weddings is a completely different genre than other types of visual work. It's also wise to avoid friends' and relatives' offers to make the photography or videography a gift, unless they are pros.

STRAIGHT TALK

Traditionally, the photographer takes portrait shots (and engagement shots, if needed), as well as candid and posed shots at the ceremony and reception. Photojournalistic shots, in which the day is recorded in a more "honest" fashion, are increasingly popular, as is a mixture of black-and-white and color photos. In addition to all the formal shots, your photographer needs to know who's essential to photograph at the ceremony, as well as specific activities — cake cutting, garter toss, toasts, etc. The videographer shoots a "movie" of your day, and tends to go for a highly edited look, or one that seems random. Videographers can shoot ceremonies and then stream them later at the reception. They make a film for you to keep and can add special effects, music, and pretty much everything else under the sun.

THE MAN DIFFERENCE

Men tend to want tons of photos and film clips, and any excuse to reapply powder or hire a stylist and look like stars. If it sounds like I'm stereotyping, then put down your makeup kit and send me an e-mail. Since gay weddings often have fewer family members than straight affairs, you can shoot less formal stuff and more candids.

WHAT EVERY 'MO NEEDS TO KNOW

When looking at photo books and videographer films, make sure you see several examples. Most vendors can find one suitable wedding to display, and that's not enough for you to make a proper assessment. • You should look at photos and videos

from straight and gay weddings, but try to assess ahead of time that the people you hire are comfortable being up close and personal with the two of you. These guys are going to be in your face — literally — when the first kiss takes place. • Make sure you see examples of their wedding photographs from start to finish, to get an idea of how they cover the entire affair. • Photographers and videographers can charge by the hour or the event. If you're trying to skimp on the budget, here's where you ask if they can work fewer hours. Since you don't want to miss the cake cutting, find out about overtime fees, and get all of this in writing. • Also, confirm that your house of worship or other site allows photography and videography. • Finally, as with any vendor who will be working on the premises, find out if they know the space. Familiarity means they'll have a better idea where to set up and where the best shots should be taken.

QUEERIES

Like any good film student, you need to ask
a couple of pertinent photography/videography questions.

Q. Can they handle the equipment?

A. You don't want to walk down an aisle and almost stumble over camera equipment. Good photographers and videographers should be savvy at assimilating into the crowd.

Q. Are you about to be in an indie film?

A. Many photographers and videographers will want you to sign a release saying they have rights to use your images for other purposes. If you're intent on maintaining your privacy, you'll have to get it in writing, and you might be charged more.

Q. What will the final take look like?

A. You will probably have lots of options on how the photos and films are produced, but go over all your choices, and don't assume you'll get anything that isn't in writing. That beautiful Oscar®-worthy film you saw when interviewing your videographer may not be part of the package you purchased. Always ask for more photographs and films, if undecided.

Q. Do the vendors know that "Night and Day" is not just a Cole Porter song?

A. Shooting in daytime is very different than nighttime, so make sure your vendors have adequate experience in the atmosphere you're choosing. If your wedding starts in the afternoon and is extending into the evening hours, and going from an inside ceremony to an outdoor affair, they have to know how to shoot indoor/outdoor as well. "I can figure it out" is not an acceptable answer.

Q. Have they met?

A. If your photographer and videographer know each other, that's one important introduction you don't need to worry about. They'll each understand how the other works, and will be able to coordinate shooting so as not to get in the way. If they don't know each other, make sure they're in contact *before* your wedding to go over all of the details.

IT MAY NOT BE OKAY FOR THE BRIDE, BUT . . .

Today, many photographers shoot photos before the ceremony, and there's wisdom in this method. You're dressed, you're still neat — and not inebriated — and you will have more time after the ceremony to change and get ready for the fun stuff. Most photographers like this idea, too. And if your mom shrieks at the thought of the groom seeing the groom before the wedding, remind her that a year ago she shrieked at the idea of the groom sleeping with the groom before Hell froze over.

MAY WE HAVE YOUR ATTENTION, PLEASE?

If you've been reading the paper lately, you've probably noticed that a lot of gay couples are submitting photos and announcements to local publications. These photos are traditionally shot a couple of months before the wedding, and many photographers will include them in the price of the package. Note, however, that not all wedding photographers shoot announcement photos. (You might also want the photo to send to family and friends.) If you're submitting photos to a newspaper, call the lifestyle editor or appropriate contact, listen carefully to the instructions, and follow them as closely as possible. Newspaper wedding announcements are much more competitive than you might think, so don't assume that the blurry iPhone photo of the two of you drunk at Gay Disney will suffice.

IN YOUR FACEBOOK

With all the social media outlets these days, it's time to make some private decisions about publicizing your affair. Decide now how much of your wedding you want shown on the Internet, and let your friends know. Some couples want to "share" every element of their wedding, while others would rather keep it in the family. If you're in the latter group, let it be known that photos of engagement parties, bachelor parties, the wedding and ceremony, and anything else where people will be snapping pictures are not to be shared online. It's not just your "friends" who are likely to view these photos; it's your friends' friends and anyone who starts tagging or copying your pictures. Privacy is much harder to control than most people think, and if that isn't enough to give you pause, consider this: most of the photos that people share will not have your stamp of approval, which can mean harsh lighting, your bad side, a shadow that looks like love handles, your bald spot, and . . . no, I didn't think I had to go on.

Fit to Be Tied

MONTH 10 — If you know you're going to be around unhealthy food (engagement parties, celebrations with loved ones), bring gum. But really good gum!

— *Joey Gonzalez*

HAND JOBS: *Select Your Invitations and Any Other Stationery*

Your invitations and stationery are considered a reflection of your taste and style. You can go with anything from DIY to flat-out formal. In today's world, people tend to be more on the minimalist side, not feeling the need to send out endless pieces of paper in a green-leaning planet. The Internet, too, has replaced some of the need for paper, especially when it comes to creating a wedding Web site and keeping people posted on news and updates. There's one thing that hasn't changed over time:

the delight people have in getting your invitation in the mail. Snail mail still has a purpose, so announce your nuptials with style, class, and fabulous penmanship.

THE PAPER CHASE

There are a lot of variations in stationery prices, as well as needs. While addressing your budget, keep in mind different options. In addition to the invitations, there are save-the-date cards, response cards, reception cards (only needed if it's at a different site than the ceremony), table and place cards, and thank-you notes. Years ago, it was considered appropriate to put the reception information on the invitation, and it would be nice to see a return to that condensed invitation. If you want to save money, be my guest and revive that tradition.

Pricewise, you can go high-end with a local stationer, or you can save some money by using a retail store. You can save even more money by making the invitations yourself. Software programs make this a practical practice, but only do it if you know you're going to have time. Calligraphy is an expensive and popular option for wedding invitations. Do not try this at home, kids, unless you're pros. Go with an expert and expect to pay expert prices. If you *really* want to go all out, have your invitations engraved, then carve into your pocketbook for the fee.

STRAIGHT TALK

For invitations, tradition calls for the hosts of the wedding (usually the bride's parents) to be listed first, followed by the bride and groom. The date goes next, then the time, place, and address. If both sets of parents are hosting the wedding, the bride's family goes first on the invite. If the bride and groom are paying for the wedding themselves, something simple like "We invite you to celebrate our love" is a great opener.

THE MAN DIFFERENCE

If any parents are paying for the wedding (or even if they're not), feel free to begin the invitation in traditional fashion. As weddings change, however, so do invitations.

Many couples, straight and gay, are considering less formal options. Some people go a "write your own vows"-type route, with openings like "Hey, we're getting hitched!" The choice is yours; just make sure all the important information is included and easy to understand. If you're hosting the wedding yourselves, listing your names alphabetically is a safe route. Not satisfied because your name is "Zimalwayslast"? Do the mature, intelligent, scientific thing: flip a coin.

WHAT EVERY 'MO NEEDS TO KNOW

Order 20 more invitations than necessary. You're going to make mistakes, so accept it now while you can still do something about it. • Did the invitations come back with the note that Alice doesn't live there anymore? People move a lot, so make sure the addresses are current. If you have any doubt, call. • Know the exact date the stationery will be delivered to you, so you have enough time to send the invitations out. • When your cards come back, proofread carefully, then proofread again. You should both participate in this process, as there's nothing worse than sending out an invitation that says you're getting married "to top a mountain." • When your RSVPs start coming in, create a checklist. Your mind is more preoccupied than you probably know, and nothing should be left to chance. • Take all invitations to the post office and mail them from there. If you can miscalculate nine inches, you can easily miscalculate the true weight of your envelopes.

CHATTY KATHY: *Create a Wedding Web Site*

Everyone creates a wedding Web site nowadays, and it's a wonderful planning tool. If you're good with computers, you can make one yourself; if not, there are plenty of gay-friendly vendors that will create it. In addition to being a site where you can post photos and talk about how you met (just don't go all Beyoncé and Jay-Z on the guests), wedding Web sites are perfect places to list your registry (without posting it on your invitation) and update all relevant information. Your wedding party and guests will love that you list dates of fittings, hotel phone numbers for reservations, directions to the ceremony and reception sites, and anything else you think is appropriate. The two of you will love the fact that, instead of bothering you guys every day, people can check the site to find out where the engagement lunch is being held. A wedding Web site is not a substitute for anything that needs to be sent via snail mail. Most important, know that some guests might not have access to or like using the Internet. They need to have their information taken care of in "old-fashioned" ways. It's essential, too, to post a phone number of a close relative or friend who can answer last-minute emergency questions.

IT'S A DRAG? *Changing Your Name*

You've dreamed all your life of becoming Mrs. Ricky Martin, and now's your chance . . . sort of. Changing your name is not nearly as common for gay men as it is for straight couples, but there are reasons for consideration. If you're having children, do you want them to have your last name or his? While kids are perhaps the most common reason to change names, other people just like the traditional aspect — not to mention any confusion about your marital status. You can take his name, he can take yours, or you can hyphenate, pick an entirely new name, or combine your two names into a hybrid moniker — yes, people do this. Whatever you decide, legally changing your name varies from state to state, so go online, or speak with a lawyer, to find out the rules.

THE HELP: *When You Need a Wedding Planner*

If you don't have the funds to hire a wedding planner, don't fret. Weddings have been planned without them for ages. If you do have extra dough, or just feel overwhelmed, consider their services. Wedding planners work best for couples who start out thinking they can handle everything, and then discover, six months into the planning, they hadn't given a thought to the catering. Sometimes, couples begin to feel daunted because of time constraints, a new job, a new location, or any other major life change. If you're considering hiring a planner, ask around and make sure you find out the different services offered. Some planners cover the entire affair, some come in as fixer-uppers, and some just show up the day of your ceremony to make sure everything's working as planned.

$ $

CHEAP TRICK
Address all envelopes yourself. It's time consuming, but it can save you a bundle and give your invitations an extra-personal look.

Chapter 4: Nine Months Ahead
WHO'S ON TOP?

- [ ] Delegate duties between the two of you
- [ ] Create your fitness and health plan
- [ ] Interview and hire the band, DJ, or both
- [ ] Personalize your wedding
- [ ] Do not skip over "Create your fitness and health plan"

ROLE-PLAY: *Delegate Duties*

Women give birth to children in nine months, so you can certainly plan a wedding in the same amount of time. To keep things going smoothly, delegate duties. Sit down in front of the computer, your iPad, or a spiral notebook and go over who's doing what. Kind of like those videos you watched in your single days, one of you gets to be the bad cop, though this time around that means making sure all contracts are signed and no one rips you off. The other gets to be the good cop, dealing with parents, friends, and anyone else whose nerves are frayed.

Chances are that one of you is better at planning, so go down the list and decide who should do what. (Flip for flowers.) One of you should handle the caterer dilemmas, and one should make sure the registry's updated. Decide who's going to schedule the cake tastings, who's in charge of legal matters, and who is going to organize writing the thank-you notes (both signatures need to be on them). If you delegate duties today, you'll have a much easier time of it when the real labor pains begin.

Fit to Be Tied

MONTH 9 — Now that you've been working out more, pay attention to the way clothes fit. The goal? Tighter in the chest and arms, and loser in the stomach. If you're not feeling that, reassess your workout plan.

— *Joey Gonzalez*

SHAPE UP: *Your Health and Fitness Plan*

Fitting into your tuxes is an important goal. Making it to your wedding without being hauled into the emergency room for exhaustion is an even more important goal. If you're both already avid gym bunnies, you're probably already scheduling in your workouts; just make sure you don't start substituting protein bars and shakes for real food. Planning a wedding is the time to get more sleep, to eat better, and to make sure you get exercise, not the other way around. If you haven't done so yet, add a fitness program into your weekly routine. (Before you say "I don't have time," remember that you'll have more energy to plan the wedding if you've gotten enough sleep, eaten right, and exercised.) Depending on what you're used to, schedule some time each day or a few times each week for cardio — long walks count. Throw out all the junk food in the fridge, and understand that the lilies versus orchids controversy can wait until the morrow.

HITTING THE RIGHT NOTES: *Select the Band, DJ, or Both*

If you think music is important to your everyday life, think of how big a part it will play at your wedding. In addition to the ceremony music, you're going to have to decide what you want for the cocktail hour and the reception. Many people also have after parties, which tend to be a bit like circuit parties, without the agony or the Ecstasy.

When choosing music, your ceremony and reception sites and themes are vital. Restaurants are probably going to frown on a large band — and they might not have much space — and houses of worship are particular about what type of music is played during a ceremony. Frequently, it's already provided. Since you have the site picked out, decide on the tone of the event. Bands are wonderful, and they keep people dancing all night. They are also loud, which doesn't work well in a loft environment or in your suburban neighborhood. DJs are terrific, too. You hear songs by the original artists, and the DJ can be a major host of the party. A third option is to hire both, and have the DJ take over when the band takes breaks. Think about who's at your wedding and the level of formality. If you've got an older crowd, do you really want a DJ playing Ke$ha's "Blow"? If your friends are "Gleeks," is the jazz quartet *really* the way to go?

STRAIGHT TALK

Most traditional ceremonies have music for the prelude, processional, ceremony, and recessional. This is often provided by the house of worship; if you want to add something, you need to formally request it. It's common to have music for the cocktail hour, and you can hire members of the reception band, or go a completely different route — hire, say, a harpist or soloist.

THE MAN DIFFERENCE

Not as many men have their ceremonies in a house of worship, and even fewer of them want "Ave Maria" played. If your wedding is being held in a less-traditional space, the

world is your musical oyster. Go with what your hearts desire, and let the music do the talking.

STAR SEARCHES

To find bands and DJs, talk to friends, ask other vendors, and do Internet searches. When interviewing, make sure the DJ you're speaking to will be the one who shows up on the day of your wedding. With bands, find out about replacements in case of emergency. Tell the band or DJ the type of songs you want, and find out how much flexibility they have. Also, let them know ahead of time about requests. If you don't want Pariah Scary, aka Mariah Carey, played at your reception, the people you hired have to be informed. All it takes is one misguided guest to get hold of a naïve DJ for there to be an endless night of Justin Bieber tunes.

WHAT EVERY 'MO NEEDS TO KNOW

Before you make any decisions on a band or DJ, find out if the venue allows it, and if it has a dance floor. (Some event companies will build one.) • Bands and DJs will usually be paid by the hour or the gig. Find out about overtime fees, and get *everything* in writing. • You will probably be expected to feed them. If your menu is three-course fantastic, you can always serve them an alternative, like pasta. • Make sure there are enough power outlets at all venues. Backup generators might be required. • Replacements are common, especially with bands. You need to have the names of any substitute musicians or DJs.

DON'T TRY THIS AT HOMO

Streisand sang at her own wedding, so if you have several Grammys® under your belt, sell out at stadiums worldwide, and have access to a teleprompter, by all means follow her lead and sing to your man. Otherwise, sit this idea out and hire a pro.

$$

CHEAP TRICKS

Find out if members of the band can play at the cocktail hour. You'll pay extra, but not nearly as much as hiring different musicians. • Don't knock the iPod idea for the cocktail hour. If you're hiring the band or DJ for only a few hours, you can save a lot by creating a perfect playlist for guests. If you don't hire a DJ, you can also set up the iPod for when the band takes breaks. And if you have a friend or relative who's great with music, and who isn't a Rockefeller, ask him or her to make a playlist as your wedding gift. That way, you all win.

QUEERIES

Here are some important questions to ask as you navigate the world of music.

Q. What's required up front?

A. Get in writing the deposit needed, as well as the cancellation policy. You'll also need to know how you are covered, should the band or DJ default.

Q. Where are you playing?

A. While hearing a CD of a group is nice, it's best to see them play live. Never crash another wedding, but find out if they're doing any local club appearances. For the DJ, make sure you get a disc of his or her performances.

Q. Need a lift?

A. If the band is not local, you might be expected to pay for their trip. This issue needs to be covered in the contract.

Q. Got protection?

A. Ask if the band is insured for accidents. If not, you might be forced to fork out the cash if an amplifier falls onto one of your guests. Get the policy information ASAP.

SINGULAR SENSATION: *Personalizing Your Wedding*

You already know the style of your wedding, the budget, and the location. Right about now you're going to be hearing a lot of "no's." Planners, caterers, and just about everyone else will have strict rules about time limits, food, outfits, music, and everything else you've been rebelling about since you and your girlfriends just wanted to have fun. To stop the doldrums from setting in, sit down with your partner and figure out personal touches. If you're having a theme, collaborate with your fiancé and vendors on the color scheme you want, and coordinate centerpieces, flowers, and linens. Depending on your site, a lot of the "extras" might *have* to be decided by the two of you. Don't finally surrender to the pink; talk to vendors about any and all personal touches, and try to implement them. Unless you've hired Martha Stewart, most vendors will want your input and will try to make your "aisle of umbrellas" work in the space. This is the time to talk about the  ice bar you've been dreaming about, or the chocolate fountain, or the mannequin centerpieces, or the Oompa Loompa–themed waiters. If something is too expensive, work with vendors on a cheaper alternative. The sky's the limit when it comes to love; reach for the stars when planning your day.

OOPS . . . ! WE DID IT AGAIN: *The Most Common Gay-Wedding Mistakes*

KNOW YOUR CROWD

When you choose your site and create a guest list, go over everyone who's invited, and make sure you haven't neglected their needs. A Splash Bar New York rehearsal dinner might not sit well with the more conservative guests, nor will the prewedding Fetish Fiesta. If you're having a beach ceremony, make sure the women (and some men) know not to wear heels and hose. Always make sure the locations you choose are handicap- and wheelchair-accessible. Late-night parties are awesome, as long as those

who go to bed at nine don't feel neglected. Yes, it's your party, but don't make other people cry. If you do have an all-night soirée, it's good to find activities for those less inclined to wake up with the sun.

POLITICAL SCIENCE

Before you prepare joint vows on the repressive nature of Maggie Gallagher and the Roman Catholic Church, consider if this is the right day for political speeches. You've no doubt witnessed those Academy Award® diatribes that put a dent in the festivities; do you want the same thing to happen on your wedding day? Far be it from me, or anyone else, to tell you what you should or should not say at your wedding; just keep in mind the potential consequences before you recite your ten-minute monologue on the dangers of watching too much Kathy Griffin.

EXCLUDING THE INCLUDED

Never assume that your conservative relatives don't want to attend your gay wedding, unless they've sent you a note saying "We don't want to attend your gay wedding." There are lots of friends and relatives who might be on your "iffy" list; try to find out through the grapevine their reaction to your nuptials. If you really want Aunt Mayberry to attend, but know that she's still sending weekly checks to Oral Roberts, have a friend or relative get the scoop. You might find that, when she learns you're getting hitched, her heart will burst out of her apron strings, just like the Grinch's did when he heard all of Whoville singing.

INCLUDING THOSE WHO EXCLUDE

On the other, less-attractive hand, the fun you have celebrating your love and commitment in front of everybody isn't always going to be contagious. Make sure those on-the-fence friends and relatives are sincere in their support before inviting them. People might attend out of a sense of duty or obligation, then spend the entire day or weekend disapproving of your sinful match. Since your true friends will do their best to shield all confrontation from you, there might be a lot of fights and tension behind the scenes. At the risk of hurting someone's feelings, or being told you're practicing the art of discrimination, do not invite bigots to your wedding. On a day of love and hope and happiness, that's like finding a worm in the wonderful apple of your eye.

MISSING THE BOAT AND THE FLOAT

Many men reading this have already been married, to each other. Gay-marriage laws have changed so much, and not always for the best, that there are guys who've been hitched in London, Toronto, and California. And now they find themselves saying, "We keep going through the legal process — when do we get to party?" Just because you've signed on the dotted line three or four years ago doesn't mean you can't have a big party now! If you never had the reception, splurge now. There's no rule that says you need to call it an anniversary party. And your friends won't feel like it's a little too late; they'll be thrilled they finally get to share the love. Register, book a band, and say your vows again. In other words, have your wedding the way you want it at anytime you want it. The laws of love never vary.

PROPOSITION GR8

I remember waking up one morning a few months after we were dating. We were lying in bed, and I forget what we were talking about, but the subject of marriage came up, and I heard myself asking Camillo if he would marry me, and he said yes. I asked if he was serious and he said yes. We didn't rush out to get married. I think we had in our minds that we would plan the ceremony/reception, but we weren't taking steps to do it. Maybe we were overwhelmed about the planning. After two and a half years, we took the commuter train to Stamford's city hall and applied for a marriage license. The following week, the two of us took the train there again and got married.

I think we just wanted to feel secure in whatever legal or social framework there is for same-sex marriage, and we didn't want to wait and save money for a ceremony and reception. But now, Camillo often brings up the subject of having a reception, so we can have a party and get gifts and celebrate our wedding in the proper manner that is due.

— TOM, MARRIED TO CAMILLO,
STAMFORD, CONNECTICUT, JUNE 9, 2009

WE'VE ONLY JUST BEGUN:
The Ten Gayest Wedding Songs Ever

Karen Carpenter's guilty-pleasure song is just one wedding song that's made the rounds more times than your best man. We've put together a list of songs so gay you won't need to throw a bouquet or purchase pink bridesmaids' dresses . . . for the guys. Granted, many of these songs are classics and make for great first-dance tunes. Before you hire the Celine Dion impersonator to sing "My Heart Will Go On," remember that, like your outfit, you don't want a song to out-gay you.

1. "Evergreen"
Barbra Streisand

WHY IT'S FOR HOMOS: It's Streisand, it's from a campy movie musical (*A Star Is Born*), and did we mention that it's Streisand?

WHY IT'S A GREAT WEDDING SONG: Let's face it, the song has nuptial legs. It's as "gorgeous" as Babs's nails, and contains sudsy lines about love being like "an easy chair" and "the morning air." Who's not going to fall in love to that?

WHY YOU MIGHT WANT TO RETHINK IT: Unless Barbra's singing it, those words sound awfully corny. It's also been done more times than Joan Rivers's face.

GAY-PLUS: Your parents and their parents know it, and you're sure to impress most of the older crowd in attendance — provided they're not Republicans.

2. "The Wind Beneath My Wings" **Bette Midler**

WHY IT'S FOR HOMOS: Hello! Have you seen Bette Midler in concert? Hello, again! Have you seen *Beaches*?

WHY IT'S A GREAT WEDDING SONG: It's one of the most inspirational ballads ever written about the person standing next to you.

WHY YOU MIGHT WANT TO RETHINK IT: It's about a woman who dies. And it pretty much killed Midler's movie career. That's two strikes . . .

GAY-PLUS: Everyone's a sucker for this tune, even those who won't admit it — which is pretty much everyone at your wedding party. Bonus points if you screen the flick at a prenuptial party, or spring for Midler tickets.

3. "Just the Way You Are"
Billy Joel

WHY IT'S FOR HOMOS: Your intended never did lose those 20 pounds or bulk up like he promised six months ago. Now's the time he really needs to hear you love him for the guy he is.

WHY IT'S A GREAT WEDDING SONG: It's slow, it's got soul, and it's even cooler than the Bruno Mars song of the same title.

WHY YOU MIGHT WANT TO RETHINK IT: Mr. Joel doesn't like to sing it anymore because he divorced the woman he wrote it for. And then he divorced the one after that, and after that. Is this the note you want to hit?

GAY-PLUS: Most singers can pull this tune off without sounding like karaoke night gone afoul. And, with all the gay-icon singers you've set up on the playlist, it's nice to have a tune that doesn't come with a remix.

4. "Dreams"
Fleetwood Mac

WHY IT'S FOR HOMOS: Stevie Nicks is a gay man trapped in a platform-boots body. (Heck, she even has a guy's name.) Chances are, it's also the song your Uncle Mike came out to that summer on Fire Island.

WHY IT'S A GREAT WEDDING SONG: No one sings like Stevie Nicks, and the haunting melody never grows old.

WHY YOU MIGHT WANT TO RETHINK IT: There's a good chance half the people in your wedding party used it for their first dance song.

GAY-PLUS: It'll give the lesbian guests a chance to whip out their shawls and take a spin around the dance floor.

5. "Magic"
Olivia Newton-John

WHY IT'S FOR HOMOS: Have you seen *Xanadu*? 'Nuff said.

WHY IT'S A GREAT WEDDING SONG: Slow, haunting, and there's even a dance remix to encourage the guests to get up on the floor.

WHY YOU MIGHT WANT TO RETHINK IT: Like I said before, it's from *Xanadu*.

GAY-PLUS: Everyone loves a pre-wedding *Xanadu* screening party. Bonus points if you invite the guests to go roller-skating!

6. "My Heart Will Go On"
Celine Dion

WHY IT'S FOR HOMOS: How many times did you watch *Titanic*? Yeah, thought so.

WHY IT'S A GREAT WEDDING SONG: Seventy-five gazillion Las Vegas ticket buyers can't be wrong.

WHY YOU MIGHT WANT TO RETHINK IT: Their hearts might go on, but the ship sinks.

GAY-PLUS: Announce that you're the king and king of the world, then watch the queens cheer you on.

7. "Your Song"
Elton John

WHY IT'S FOR HOMOS: You're kidding, right?

WHY IT'S A GREAT WEDDING SONG: It's not about money or material items; it's about him.

WHY YOU MIGHT WANT TO RETHINK IT: Elton probably sang it at Rush's wedding. Ewwww!

GAY-PLUS: Wear platform shoes, huge glasses, and lots of glitter. In other words, drag out your Gay Pride clothes!

8. "Teenage Dream"
Katy Perry

WHY IT'S FOR HOMOS: It's new, it's now, it's trendy, and he does think you're funny when you tell the punchline wrong.

WHY IT'S A GREAT WEDDING SONG: We all want to feel that first crush come alive again, no matter what our age.

WHY YOU MIGHT WANT TO RETHINK IT: Three words: Russell Brand divorce.

GAY-PLUS: After this song, have the DJ go right into "Firework," and light up sparklers all around the reception site.

9. "Crazy for You"
Madonna

WHY IT'S FOR HOMOS: Okay, this is getting old.

WHY IT'S A GREAT WEDDING SONG: Not too corny, not too "done," not too unhip. Like the two of you, it's just cool enough.

WHY YOU MIGHT WANT TO RETHINK IT: Playing a Madonna song is liable to get your guests debating whether she's the Queen of Everything, or a clear sign that the end is near.

GAY-PLUS: On the other hand, hearing a Madonna song's going to lead smart guests to beg the DJ to play everything from "Holiday" to "Vogue." You'll be there all night.

10. "1 + 1"
Beyoncé

WHY IT'S FOR HOMOS: The gays don't like to add, and Beyoncé made it easy for you.

WHY IT'S A GREAT WEDDING SONG: Big, elaborate, dramatic; just like the two of you.

WHY YOU MIGHT WANT TO RETHINK IT: The song disappeared so quickly I don't even think Beyoncé remembers the lyrics to it. Good luck finding a DJ that has it in stock or a singer who knows the words.

GAY-PLUS: It's the perfect segue into the much more fun "Single Ladies (Put a Ring on It)."

Chapter 5: Eight Months Ahead
YOU BETTER WORK

- ☐ Interview and hire a florist
- ☐ Register for gifts
- ☐ Start writing thank-you notes
- ☐ Choose the women's formalwear
- ☐ If either one of you is wearing a dress, get it now
- ☐ Delegate jobs to the wedding party
- ☐ Plan something special as a favor to your friends
- ☐ Sign your prenuptial agreements
- ☐ Accept the fact that fuchsia and groomzilla are not attractive colors on you

At this stage in the game, it's good to talk about timelines. While we've picked different months for different components, there's wiggle room. Some couples hire the band a year in advance; some people figure out the flowers right away. As you whip through your checklists, just understand that some tasks are more urgent than others. As with every "chore," the sooner you get it over with, the more time for fun. Generally, vendors will agree and advise you to sign on the dotted line immediately. Don't rush into anything because you feel pressured, and don't plan too far in advance. Those amazing circus performers you've decided on might not want to be booked up a year ahead of time, in case Donald Trump gets married again. Keep things in perspective and keep moving. You're on the right track.

PETAL PUSHER: *Finding the Right Florist*

Florists are a dime a dozen, er, roses, so it's just a matter of finding the one who works for you. Some people are crazy for blooms, and they want them all over the ceremony site, the reception area, the tables, the outfits, and pretty much anywhere the eye can see. Other guys are more staid when it comes to stems, keeping them minimalistic in favor of a more sleek affair. There's no rule about how much flora you need at your wedding — you could skip them altogether if you wish. (If you do pull that one off, send me the photos so I can see how you managed!) Pick your stems according to your needs and budget, and everything will grow just right.

STAR SEARCH

To find your florist, think outside the pot. In addition to asking friends and relatives and searching online, think of all the great flowers you've seen. If there's any benefit or dinner you've been to that had fantastic flowers, find out who the florist was; ditto a restaurant with a great display. Talk to your green-thumb friends about whom they trust. Think back to all the flowers you've received over the past couple of years, and inquire about the florist who sent the roses that didn't wilt before they hit the vase. If you live in New Jersey, but you know a great flower shop back home in Iowa, call and ask if they have suggestions in your area.

WHAT EVERY 'MO NEEDS TO KNOW

Local flowers are almost inevitably cheaper than out-of-season blooms, so make lists of first, second, and third choices. • Sneezing can ruin those heartfelt vows; avoid flowers you're allergic to — also, talk to your wedding party about any allergies they have. • Sunflowers are lovely, but they might make table conversation a bit difficult if you use them as centerpieces; keep stems low enough so that people can see over them.

• Check out the florist's shop; his displays will give you an idea of his taste — it's like checking out someone's living room to see if you like the furniture. • If you like the florist, but aren't quite sold on him as your vendor of choice, have him make up a bouquet to see if it suits your fancy. • Which leads us to the next big decision . . .

STRAIGHT TALK

Traditionally, the bride has a bouquet, and the women in the wedding party have smaller versions. Boutonnieres are standard for the groom and the other guys — best man, groomsmen, ushers, and ring bearer. The groom's boutonniere should stand out from the other blooms. Corsages are given to mothers, grandmothers, and female attendants. Flowers are commonly used at the ceremony site (sometimes as aisle runners or on pews), and they are standard as centerpieces and around the reception site.

THE MAN DIFFERENCE

Those bouquets are expensive, and you're going to save big bucks if you go without. But, hey, if you've been dreaming of throwing that bouquet since you were a little girlfriend, by all means get one or two. If you have females in the wedding party, it's nice to get them flowers. If you think bouquets clash with the men's buds, single blooms are a nice touch.

QUEERIES

Here are some looming, blooming questions you need to ask your florist.

Q. Do the flowers go with the color scheme?

A. Always make sure florists know your colors and themes, so they'll have great suggestions as to what flowers work best with your vision. Also, ask about substitutes in case certain flowers are unavailable at the last minute. If you know nothing about flowers, this is the time when you should make sure the florist understands your wedding vision.

Q. Your place or mine?

A. Ask if the florist knows the wedding spot. If so, he will have a better grasp of where to put blooms, as well as ways to save money. If he doesn't know the ceremony site, insist he check it out ahead of time.

P.S. You don't want pollen on your clothes, so double-check to make sure the blooms won't stain on your parade.

WHO'S THE GROWER AND WHO'S THE SHOWER?

You need to know which florist you'll be dealing with — it might not be the person you meet at the shop. You'll also need to know if flowers are going to be set up at the site or just dropped off. Find out who the backup person is, and get all names on the contract. If your florist is not going to set up, designate this job to a trusted friend or relative. Don't be fooled into thinking you'll have the time to play flower coordinator on the day of your wedding.

'TIS THE SEASON?

If the flowers you want are already blooming locally, you're going to save a considerable sum compared to having them sent from halfway around the world.

> **Planting Help.** Arrange to have your flowers sent to a hospital or charitable organization when your ceremony is over. If that doesn't work out, tell everyone to take them home . . . after you leave the site.

CHEAP TRICKS

Plants are cheaper than flowers; you can spread them around the site to save money and incorporate them into centerpieces. • Speaking of centerpieces, you don't have to use flowers; anything from coins to seashells to candles will do — but check out the last idea to make sure you're actually saving money. • One may be the loneliest number in song, but not for arrangements. Go with a stark theme, use fewer blooms, and save more money. • If you have your ceremony near a holiday, like Christmas or Halloween, a lot of the ornamentation might already be provided. Ask the site manager what's staying planted. • To really save money, find a site that's already decorated with hearty plants and flowers, or have your ceremony in a garden area.

Of all the wedding customs that bring the most "pause" to gay men (next to marrying a woman, of course), registering for gifts tops the list. Most men love presents, but there's a feeling among many couples that it's too traditional for a gay wedding. Another issue is age and income; since a lot of gay males get married older than straight couples and have two incomes, they feel as if asking for gifts is self-centered or greedy. On the other hand, there's probably a lot of men reading this and thinking, "Screw that — I want the gifts!"

Wherever you are on the spectrum, registering for gifts is a smart idea even if you're not thrilled about receiving another martini set. For starters, your loved ones will want to give you presents, and without a registry, they're on their own. That may not always be desirable for some of your more taste-challenged friends.

STRAIGHT TALK

You get engaged, you set the date for the wedding, and Mom tells a thousand of your closest friends where you're registered. It's considered bad form to list your registry information on wedding invitations. If you don't want gifts, it's still an etiquette no-no to say so on your invitations.

THE MAN DIFFERENCE

If you are getting married after you've been together for some time, registering for traditional items might be impractical. No one's going to be upset if you announce that gifts are not wanted (and people aren't quick to judge if you break the rule and say so on the invitations), but some guests will buy you a present regardless. If you prefer to be cause worthy in your registry, many gay-rights organizations have registries. Obviously, you can also have money donated to any charity you wish to support. Also, don't think that just because you're over 30 and living together, you can't register at Tiffany's or another traditional place. Most major retailers have same-sex or non-gender-specific registries, and are thrilled and accustomed to working with gift-hungry men. A lot of online wedding sites allow you to combine your registry information when they create your Web site.

WHAT EVERY 'MO NEEDS TO KNOW

In an online world, registering is easier than ever. You can fill out all the paperwork and register for pretty much everything you need, without leaving your computer. Your guests can buy you wedding gifts without getting out of their chairs, too. Two caveats: it's helpful to get an actual look at specialty products, so take a visit to the store. Also, not everyone's plugged in, so there should be an 800 number listed for anyone who needs to call to buy you a gift. • While your registry will include an address for mailing gifts to you, people will still show up at your wedding with packages. Be gracious, and make sure you've set up a gift table. (Open gifts *after* people leave.) • If you prefer cash, have people spread the news the same way they would about where you're registered — via word of mouth. • If you're having a large wedding, consider registering at two spots: a large store and one that's more customized. • Check your registry on a regular basis and make sure it's updated. • Since there's a good chance that your friends and relatives will have a range of incomes, register for big and small items. • No matter what you ask for or where you register, in the end it's a little like your birthday — some people will always get you what you didn't ask for.

SUPPORT GROUPS

Much has been written about organizations that are "gay friendly" yet contribute tons of money to antigay politicians and causes. In order to avoid supporting groups that don't always practice the tolerance they preach, do your research. Contact gay-rights organizations in your area, and ask them for a list of gay-friendly companies (if you

Fit to Be Tied

MONTH 8 — If you're on the heavier side, wear black when you work out. After all, it's only a funeral for your fat.
—*Joey Gonzalez*

can't find one posted on their site). You can also do a search for gay vendors, and create your registry that way — the same goes for searching for honeymoon hotels and destinations. Also, ask your politically savvy friends who's on the "bad and good lists" — most of them will know the drill.

SPEED DATE

If you're registering for something big, like a trip to Australia, do it right after you've set the date, so guests can start contributing immediately. For more conventional registries, don't jump the gun if your wedding is more than a year off. Items change and are discontinued. If you're having a very small wedding, and aren't crazy about gifts, you can put this task off for two more months; know, however, that people will inquire as soon as you've set the date. Another advantage to registering early is that it helps the people who aren't attending your wedding to get your gift taken care of and move on with their lives — seriously.

A NOTE ON THANK-YOU NOTES

For gifts that arrive before the wedding, send out thank-you notes within two weeks. For gifts that arrive the day of or after, you should send out notes within a month of the day received (add a week or so if you're honeymooning). Etiquette dictates that guests have a year to send a gift, so don't bitch over brunch if your gym buddy's only package was in his too-tight tux.

FEMALE TROUBLE: *Women's Formalwear*

For most guys, the formalwear can wait until four months before the wedding. Tuxes and suits aren't that complicated to find. However, if there are women in your wedding party, or if one of you wants to wear a dress, tackle this step now.

DRESS YOU UP

Want to be married in a gown? You can try an independent bridal store or go off-the-rack or vintage. There will probably be some alterations needed, so make sure the site has a seamstress. Like all your girlfriends, don't buy a dress that's too tight; while dieting is a great goal before your wedding, it's not guaranteed to work. You can take a dress in, but "out" is a lot harder than when you did it yourself. For accessories, hit

vintage stores, department stores, or Mom's closet — you know, like the old days. A wedding is, to a certain degree, the final step in announcing to the world that you love and are committed to men. If that declaration includes wearing an extravagant ball gown or a shimmering A-line, make the most of it. If there is hesitation or lack of enthusiasm on the part of any store, manufacturer, or human being, move on to the people and places who love you for who you are.

WONDER WOMEN: *Dressing the Girls*

If either one of you is having a maid or matron of honor for the ceremony, or you are having female attendants or flower girls, you need to plan their outfits. Chances are, this is going to be an easier task than for your

straight female friends when they get married. If you two grooms are wearing suits or tuxes, the women should have outfits that complement your look but are uniquely their own. For a gay wedding, what this means is that if you're both wearing white linen, the maid of honor probably shouldn't don a flaming-red dress. If you want to go with traditional bridesmaids' dresses, start searching now. You can pick a designer and fabric, and let the women go wild with styles and accessories — remember, different styles allow women to hide their flaws and show off their assets. A more popular option is to tell attendants the style and formality of your wedding, and let them choose their own outfits. If there is more than one woman in your wedding party, they'll need to coordinate. I'm going to go out on a limb here and offer up one piece of "controversial" advice: If you want your female friends to love you even more than they do now, let them pick something they'll love to wear to your wedding, and something they will be thrilled to wear again. That's wedding progress.

THEY BETTER WORK: *Delegate Jobs to the Wedding Party*

Now that you know who's in the wedding party, decide what you want them to do. Like your drag getup on Halloween, less is often more. Before turning your best man and maid of honor and parents and siblings and 3,000 closest Facebook friends into slaves, remember that they have lives outside of your wedding. If someone volunteers to help pick out tuxedos, fantastic. If no one volunteers to arrange your honeymoon airfare, hotel, and on-site manis and pedis, that's because it's your job. Sit down with your partner and go over areas where you really need help, and then discuss who's offered and who's up to the task. If your best man lives near your wedding site,

and he volunteers, have him check out the parking situation that's still causing a problem. If you need someone to help you pick out suits, choose one friend to go with you. Contrary to what you're thinking, seven gay men discussing how you look in Prada will not result in seven helpful tips. More than likely, it will lead to you crying and deciding you're too fat and ugly to get married, or live.

BACHELOR (PARTY) NUMBER ONE AND TWO

Your loved ones have already thought about parties, and they might already have planned an engagement party or casual cocktail affair. Bachelor parties and showers are a tad different for men than women, for two reasons — um, don't make me explain. Technically, the groom and groom don't plan the parties or host them, since they are often surprise events. However, if you don't want either one of these parties, let everyone know. If you do, throw a few hints their way.

Are You a Groomzilla?

Ten Ways to Know If You've Gone Over the Top

1. You fire your dog as ring bearer because he keeps forgetting his lines.

2. You refer to yourself as "Master" and the guys in your wedding party as "Slaves" — and are clueless as to any irony this might entail.

3. Martha Stewart is calling *you* for tips.

4. Three words: rainbow-colored groomsmen.

5. You no longer think the wedding in *Mamma Mia* is gay enough.

6. Your mother now has an unlisted phone number.

7. Your ringtone is the "Wedding March."

8. You refer to every royal-family wedding as "amateur hour."

9. You took your best friend off speed dial so you'd have room for "Place-Card Feng-Shui Coordinator."

10. Your fiancé secretly wishes he could be marrying someone a bit less obsessed with wedding planning — like one of the Kardashians.

Concerning bachelor parties: if you've dreamed of having the whole kit and caboodle with big drinks, big strippers, and tiny G-strings, go ahead — just clear it with your fiancé. He might want to do the same with his friends. You can also combine the affair, but the stripper part might be a little eepy-cray. Joint parties are becoming increasingly popular, and they can be anything from a guys' night out to theater to cocktails to spa treatments. Let your wedding party know what you prefer, and make sure they understand the finances of all the guests (everyone is supposed to chip in, regardless of who hosts). If anyone in your wedding party abstains from alcohol, don't plan a wine-tasting trip. (He's just being nice when he volunteers to be the designated driver.) If you are planning any sort of boozefest, do not have the party the night before your wedding. Hangovers belong in buddy flicks, not when you're reciting vows in front of your best buddies.

RETURN THE FAVORS: *Treating Your Wedding Party*

At some point in all the excitement over you, you, and you, you need to remember how much work your wedding party is putting into your affair. In addition to periodically telling them how much their support means to you, show your love. Take everyone involved out to lunch or dinner, and keep your wedding off-topic. It's common to plan a cocktail party or weekend getaway, or some other great adventure. You don't, however, need to spend half your budget making a grand gesture of thanks. Inviting everyone over for drinks is a fantastic way of saying "thank you" without breaking the bank.

SEPARATION ANXIETY: *Prenuptial Agreements*

No one likes to talk about prenups, just like no one likes to talk about wills — by the way, have you made yours yet? Get the prenup over with now, so you never have to deal with it again. Should your marriage be legal, it's essential to have a prenuptial agreement, and to use separate lawyers. While not as pressing, consult with lawyers about a prenuptial agreement if you are entering into a civil union or domestic partnership — in other words, anything legal. Don't ignore your partner; talk to him first. The subject may make one or the other of you (or both) a little anxious, but it's the grown-up thing to do. Prenuptials are there to protect your children and assets, not just in the case of divorce, but in terms of what happens after you're gone. It doesn't mean you think things won't work out; it's just about preparing for every eventuality, even those worst-case scenarios that you swear will never happen. Make sure your fiancé understands that that's the spirit in which you're approaching this bit of "housekeeping." After you've spoken with him privately, arrange to have a four-person discussion with your lawyers, who'll be able to answer any questions the two of you may have. Resolve all issues today, so you can start your new life!

HEART TO HEART:
Party Hearty

After we'd been hosting all night, my best friend came over and said, "Your husband wants to spend some time with you." He was sitting at the bar with a drink. We both realized that we'd done everything right — greeting people, cake cutting, toasts — but we weren't having fun. We decided that, at that point, it was our party, our *one* wedding, and we were going to have a *blast*. If something went wrong, who cares? I always tell guys getting married to remember to enjoy yourself. It's your night.

—ANDREW IRVING, MARRIED TO STEPHEN SHEPARD, MASSACHUSETTS, 2009

Chapter 6: Seven Months Ahead
TWO FOR THE ROAD

- [ ] Start planning your honeymoon
- [ ] Update travel documents
- [ ] Schedule your annual physical
- [ ] Book rooms for guests and research airfare
- [ ] Organize activities for your guests
- [ ] Rent all ceremony and reception supplies
- [ ] Add any special religious elements you choose
- [ ] Practice your honeymoon night!

TO THE MOON: *Planning Your Honeymoon*

Not so long ago, when straight people in love thought of honeymoons, they imagined hotel rooms looking over Niagara Falls, quick jaunts to Las Vegas, or getaways on a gorgeous Caribbean island or in Hawaii. Funny, the more things change, the more they stay the same. Today, gay couples are welcome in hotels around those waterfalls, Vegas, island destinations, and even Disney World®. Where you decide to spend your honeymoon is entirely up to you, of course, and your options are as amazing as you are.

What has changed about honeymoons, gay and straight, is that couples often take them a few days after the wedding (so they can relax first and take care of important matters), and some put them off for months. Jobs, finances, children — all these factors have changed the

logistics of honeymoon travel. Whatever you decide, this is a good time to start making plans.

STRAIGHT OR GAYBORHOOD?

If you spend all your vacation time hitting Provincetown, Fire Island, the Russian River, and Michele Bachmann's husband's office, there's a good chance you're going to want to book a very gay honeymoon. That could mean a gay cruise or a Key West bungalow or a bed-and-breakfast in the Castro. You'll be among your "own," and you're never going to have second thoughts about holding hands on starry nights. The only potential drawback is that you're probably not going to be the only guy giving your husband looks. Make sure you're comfortable enough to handle the flirtations so soon after your wedding. If you decide to book a clothing-optional room in a warm climate, know that half those guys wouldn't notice a wedding band if it hit them in the face.

For many of you, your honeymoon is that time to travel to destinations you've never seen, or to return to some glorious spot where you shared a birthday, anniversary, or holiday together. However, when traveling abroad or in a more "hetero" environment, you'll want to find out — in advance — how gay friendly your hotel and the surrounding areas really are. In addition to talking to the people at the hotel, and your friends and colleagues who know the area, look into the International Gay & Lesbian Travel Association (IGLTA). The IGLTA can let you know about the level of gay friendliness of hotels and destinations around the world. It's a wonderful resource and can save you a lot of time and hassle.

WHAT EVERY 'MO NEEDS TO KNOW

Travel agents can find discount packages that might escape you otherwise. Even though they seem like a relic of your parents' generation, don't disqualify them. • Wherever you stay, don't be shy. Tell them it's your honeymoon when you book; you might get an upgrade, a bottle of Champagne, or some other special treat. • Uncle Sam's resorts want you! Gay travelers are huge business these days, so expect to be greeted with open arms when you book — and if not, go AWOL and find a place that *does* want you. • Guess what? You've just exchanged vows and entered a union that's based on compromise. If you're both dead set on different destinations, flip a coin (or just flip), and pick the second destination for your next big trip.

PROTECTIVE MEASURES

If you are unseasoned travelers, or just think you're going to forget everything in the midst of wedding chaos, follow a few tips on how to make your honeymoon safe and sound.

Documents. If your passports are out of date, renew them now. Even if you're traveling within the United States, a passport can be a lifesaver if you get into any sort of jam, lose your driver's license, or decide at the last minute to hop on over to Mexico for a day. Besides, you're eventually going to need a current passport, so you might as well take care of it today. Check to see if the country you're visiting requires a visa.

Love in Vein. Contact the Centers for Disease Control about any shots needed for your trip, and schedule now. While you're at it, make sure you book your annual physical. Necessary medications should be taken on your carry-on (not in a checked bag) in case of lost luggage. Keep your doctor's information with you — it will come in handy if you should lose your supply of important meds.

Phone It In. Find out your mobile carrier's plan for out-of-country service, and make sure you switch. Phone calls, e-mails, and texts are outrageously expensive once you've left the United States.

Buy It Now. It's always nice to have an excuse to shop, and your honeymoon is a pretty good reason. Depending on where you're going, you might need a lot of different clothes. Take care of it now, so you're not running to H&M the day before your wedding. Also, as you get closer to the date, stock up on items like sunscreen and mini toiletries. Yes, you can find them at your destination, and yes, you'll spend a ton more money that way.

Take It Off. Now that you've shopped, leave half of it behind. Overpacking for your honeymoon is going to leave you lugging around bags during your trip, and then not having room to bring stuff home. When in doubt, leave it. You can always buy that floppy hat at your final destination.

Nice Tip. Tip rules vary around the world, which means you've got to do your homework. Many spots include a gratuity in restaurants. Also, since some countries think it's an affront to give too big a tip (I know — it boggles me, too), so ask ahead of time. When it comes to tipping your maid, do it each day, not at the end of your stay. It's an easy way to get better service.

$$

GROUP SCENES: *Booking Rooms and Transportation for Your Guests*

If 20 people are attending your wedding, and all of them work in your office, booking rooms isn't much of a chore. For most couples, however, ceremonies mean a lot of out-of-towners coming in from far-off places. Many of them will be flying, and most will need a place to stay. Etiquette dictates that you're not required to pay for transportation or hotels, and that you don't even need to be helpful in finding your guests a place to stay. Common courtesy dictates that if you don't try to make the experience easier for your guests, you're a douche bag.

Start booking rooms as soon as you can, and let hotels know how many guests you're expecting. Most sites will give you a discount for a big reservation, and it will only get more expensive the longer you put if off. Depending on the size of your wedding, you might have to (or want to) book a few different spots. If so, do your best to bunk people who know one another in the same locale. You can mix it up a bit, but think of it like a mini seating chart.

Plane fares are often cheaper when you book large groups, too. If you don't have any luck in that area, or it's a waste of time because people are coming from so many different places, you can search for the best airfares, and send the information along via the phone or e-mail, or on your wedding Web site. Guests will appreciate not having to spend their Saturday on Hotwire.com® looking for the best way to get to your ceremony. All guests need detailed instructions on how to reach their lodgings once they've arrived at your city. You can pick them up, have friends pick them up, arrange for limos or taxis, or give them a bus schedule (good luck not pissing off friends with this last choice).

PAY IT FORWARD

Paying for any portion of a guest's travel is not required. Should you wish to splurge on your best man's hotel suite, pay for other wedding-party members as well. It's not polite to single out certain people and give them favors. There are smaller ways you can help, such as providing transportation to and from airports; once again, just make sure everyone gets equal treatment.

BAGGAGE CLAIMS

Everyone's a sucker for a gift bag, and it's a great way to make out-of-towners feel at home. You can go really expensive and place theater tickets inside, or keep it cheap and provide some chocolates and a list of great restaurants in the area. Your friends and relatives have spent a lot of money to come see you, have taken time off from

Fit to Be Tied

MONTH 7 — Cardio *and* weights are equally important. Don't be a skinny fatty or a chub-muscle monster (pure bulk doesn't look great in suits).

—*Joey Gonzalez*

work and their regular plans, and are here to support you. A cute little gift bag waiting for them when they get to their hotel is going to bring a huge smile to their face. Talk to hotels about gift-bag suggestions. Do an Internet search, ask your florist for recommendations, or contact any nearby arts-and-crafts store.

DAY TRIPPERS: *Planning Events for Your Guests*

If your affair is short and sweet, and mostly local, guests will pretty much show up, have fun, and leave. Should you be planning on a weekend affair or expecting lots of out-of-town guests, it's nice to schedule activities for them and/or let them know what's happening in the area. While the wedding party is going to be busy, think about the ones not invited to the rehearsal dinner and not involved in any of the work. In addition to any goodies you give to win over your crowd, provide them with a printed-out list of restaurants, shows, museums, historic sites, and gyms (and post all this on your Web site). Also, consider coordinating group events. You can opt for ridiculous fun, and arrange a bowling excursion or a softball game — yes, men can be cheerleaders — or you can plan something more ambitious, like paddleboarding or bicycle riding or whatever the local landscape offers. Heck, those straight friends of yours might love to see the local drag show. Use what the surrounding environment offers and turn their stay into a real Out Adventure. Another plus: the after-wedding brunch, even if it's just Bloody Marys and bagels!

PRODUCT PLACEMENT: *Rental Information*

Before you check off "booking the site" on your to-do list, make sure you've covered all rentals that need to be taken care of. Ask your site managers, caterer, and florist about any essentials that you'll need to borrow. For your reception, this could be tables, chairs, table runners, even kitchen equipment. Never assume anything is taken care of, which could also mean wineglasses and other dinnerware. If you're celebrating at your house or a friend's, you might need a tent, Porta-Potties (they look almost classy these days), even an outdoor heater. Renting equipment is not a complicated procedure, as long as you plan ahead. You can do a search for all party supplies, and you should ask vendors whom they recommend. This is an area where you can haggle and bargain shop.

HOLY HOMOS! HOW RELIGIOUS CAN YOU GET?
Adding Special Elements

For some of you, adding any element of religion into your ceremony would be like inviting Arnold Schwarzenegger to speak about fidelity or, well, anything. By now you've probably already made your peace with God, or said your good-byes, so decide on any religious touches you'd like and seek them out.

THE FATHER, THE SON, AND THE HOLY NOT ON YOUR LIFE

Catholic boys might start too late, and they're likely going to get a gay blessing later than that. There are tons of Catholic priests (well, duh), but most dioceses forbid condoning gay weddings. You're also unlikely to find a church in your area willing to open up the doors for your Big Gay Mass. That said, if you are working with a nondenominational minister, ask him or her about any Catholic touches that can be added. It's a little like having your own personal Jesus, but you might get a prayer or blessing and a rosary or two. Like most faiths, however, you can also go online and look for denominations willing to add religious touches to your wedding.

OY, VEIL

The Jewish faith is all over the place when it comes to gay weddings, and you probably know what your rabbi's position is. Many couples incorporate the *ketubah* (an often poetic document outlining the responsibility of the marriage partners to one another) into the ceremony, and a simple Internet search will bring up dozens of same-sex-ketubah designs. Gay couples can stand under the *chuppah* (the wedding canopy), and can even have a gay version of "Sunrise, Sunset" sung at their ceremony, thanks to the original *Fiddler on the Roof* lyricist, Sheldon Harnick, who has tweaked the words of this classic wedding song so that there's now one for gay couples and one for lesbians. What a *mentsch*! As Tevye himself knew, traditions evolve. The Reform branch of Judaism is very accepting regarding same-sex couples. Talk to an officiant about any and all customs and traditions you'd like to include.

AND THE REST . . .

Whether you're Protestant, Southern Baptist, Buddhist, Muslim, or a Wiccan, there's a chance you will find obstacles to your gay wedding. However, there's a bigger chance that, if you ask around and do your homework, you can find ways to incorporate religious elements into your wedding. It can't be stressed enough how important it is to talk to couples who've been there, and to speak to gay-friendly clergy.

PRAY IT FORWARD

Etiquette dictates that your officiant's transportation and lodgings should be paid for (as well as his or her spouse's). The officiant should also be invited to the rehearsal dinner. In lieu of a fee, most officiants require a "donation" to their house of worship. If you're working with an officiant not affiliated with your church, temple, or synagogue, the fee will be much greater. Find out everything up front.

Chapter 7: Six Months Ahead
WHERE'S THE PARTY?

- [ ] Personalize your ceremony and reception to suit your style
- [ ] Mind your pooch
- [ ] Choose your cakes
- [ ] Purchase gifts for the wedding party and each other
- [ ] Assure your fiancé that the cake tasting did not make him fat . . . then have him say the same to you

VIVE LA DIFFÉRENCE!
What Makes a Same-Sex Ceremony Unique

You're halfway there, and half your friends are thinking, "So, um, will there be a father-son dance?" The other half is wondering who's walking you down the aisle. You're not thinking at all — you're waiting to show off your cha-cha skills for the first dance! As gay weddings progress, couples are adopting some of the same traditions and formality associated with straight weddings, but giving them their own distinct spin. Nowadays, it's not just your suit that may need a few alterations — in this chapter, we'll tackle a few of the customs that might need to be tailored to your taste.

THE CEREMONY

Most gay men have attended enough straight weddings to know how a wedding works, whether it's very formal, very religious, or secular-casual. The main issue gay men face is the who-walks-with-you-down-the-aisle question.

In Christian weddings, Dad walks his daughter, and in Jewish ceremonies, both parents share the honors. Let your own philosophy dictate your approach. Remember, you're not the poster wedding child for any faith except the one that involves love, so change the "rules" to whatever you feel is appropriate. If Dad wants to walk you down the aisle, fantastic. If not, choose a different loved one. Another

common route is for you and your groom to walk down together, supporting each other in this brand-new chapter of your lives. Talk to your officiant, talk to your partner, and, like the song says, "You'll Never Walk Alone."

THE RECEIVING LINE

If your wedding is large, a receiving line is a great way for everyone to congratulate you after the vows, and to quickly say hello. It's also your chance to thank them for coming. If your ceremony is being held in a house of worship, the line usually forms at the exit. Should there be no space, or you need to vacate quickly (due to another wedding party, or to take photos), the line is formed at the entrance to the reception site.

STRAIGHT TALK

Traditionally, whoever is hosting the wedding heads the line, followed by the second family (generally, the groom's). After that, it's the bride and groom, her honor attendant, and the bridesmaids.

THE MAN DIFFERENCE

Conventional receiving-line protocol isn't going to make a whole lot of sense when it comes to *your* wedding, so go with your gut and have the most important people in the line. If your parents are involved, have them both next to you, then add the members of the wedding. Tradition also dictates that fathers and honor attendants can sit this one out, and that's up to you. If you're worried about a time crunch, thin the line out or see if you can get some Champagne to be served. Be aware, too, that many sites won't allow you this option.

THE RECEPTION

Gay and straight receptions are similar in a lot of ways, so there aren't that many changes from standard operating procedure that you'll need to make. Here, it's probably the

songs and dances that you need to revisit during the planning process (see "The Ten Gayest Wedding Songs Ever" on pages 74–75). Other than that, if you're having a master of ceremonies (DJ, band leader, or drag queen), he or she introduces all the members of the wedding party as they enter, starting with the attendants, leading up to the parents, and then annoucing the two of you. A formal introduction is entirely optional, and less-formal weddings often don't include it. However you arrive at your reception, do so within an hour of the ceremony. Guests will get antsy waiting for the groom and groom and feel uncomfortable eating and mingling too much. For this reason, many guys opt to take as many photos as possible before the ceremony, and book sites that are close together.

STRAIGHT TALK

After the first dance between bride and groom comes the father-daughter dance. This is followed by the groom's dance with the mothers.

THE MAN DIFFERENCE

It's wonderful if your dad wants to dance with you guys. If that's uncomfortable or impossible, many grooms opt to have their first dance with each other and then invite everyone onto the floor. Do urge your attendants to get people on their feet — or do it yourself. Should you want to include a groom-mother dance, make sure you're not sending out a signal that Dad doesn't approve of your union. Politically speaking, it makes the most sense to have both parental dances, or none at all.

TOSS-UP

Many straight couples (and wedding guests) deplore the wedding toss, both for its rather antiquated message that the lucky girl who catches it will be married next, and because it's just plain corny. Others love it. For two guys, no one's going to be surprised if you skip the ritual. Should you want to throw the love, but don't think a bouquet is the right way to go, you can throw a tie, a boutonniere, or any other wedding item that isn't going to crush a guest's skull.

JUST TOAST

The best man gives the first toast at most weddings, so go this route if it suits you (a woman attendant can also do the honors). If you're not having attendants, or simply don't want to single out any particular person as "best," it makes sense to designate someone to start the toasting process. People are going to want to wish you well, and most will feel uncomfortable starting the process. The DJ or band leader usually announces that the toasts will commence. If you're going very casual, feel free to walk over to your toastmaster or toastmistress and let him or her know when it's time to begin.

TOASTED

You know your buds better than anyone, but do encourage any and all guests (and yourselves) not to make drunken toasts. They're funny on film, but not so much in real life. Anyone who's giving a prepared toast should rehearse it and keep it fairly short; it's okay to hold a piece of paper if nerves are getting the best of you. The friend or relative who gives you a toast should reward himself by drinking *after* he's told the gathered crowd how you got him through his three-month breakup with that Randy Blue star. That's when the tears and the drops can fall.

SERIOUSLY?

Not everyone is on board with the reality of gay weddings, so make sure you let the guests understand the meaning of this momentous event. Start by indicating the dress code on invitations (black tie, cocktail attire, casual dress), and stay on the, er, straight path all the way through the reception. Whether or not your marriage is legal, your love and commitment are valid. You don't need to think "formal" so much as "official" in your planning. Decide how you want to be addressed (as "husbands," "spouses," or "partners"), and have the person in charge of the affair introduce you to the crowd that way. The name situation is probably confusing for your guests and friends, so start earlier, having your new titles listed on the Web site, and making sure Mom, Dad, relatives and friends know. People will ask, because they want to be as correct as you are. A huge part of the reason men are going the formal route these days is because it says "real wedding." Bands and DJs, table cards and place cards, cake cutting, favors, and exiting the site in style all say, "We're here, we're queer, we're the couple of the year."

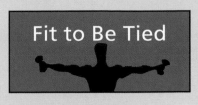

Fit to Be Tied

MONTH 6 — A workout without goals is like a broken pencil . . . pointless. If you don't have a specific plan, talk to trainers or your in-shape friends about what you'd like to achieve. Involve various forms of interval cardiovascular, strength training, and flexibility, as they are equally important.

—*Joey Gonzalez*

ANIMAL PLANET: *Pets or Peeves?*

Here's a news flash: your dog really doesn't know it's your wedding, and might be happier parking it in the dog run. Having cherished animals take part in your big day is understandable; you love the tykes, and you know they love you. There's nothing wrong with incorporating the pooch or the puss or another creature, great or small, into your affair. However, there are precautions that have to be taken. First off, chances are they're not going to cooperate as ring bearer, and they may just lift their leg at the whole event. Dogs are the most common animals to include, but make sure allergies are not going to cause problems with the wedding party. Check ahead to see if the site allows them, and find a responsible person to make sure they have constant water and aren't left in the hot sun or frightened by the crowd. Do not make an animal wear a too-tight outfit, or one that constricts his or her breathing (if you do dress your pet, find an animal-friendly site or store that specializes in animalwear). Another important note: keep Fido or Fidette away from all candy and human food that people may drop at the reception. Remember, chocolate cake may be yummy to you, but it can be deadly to your dog. It might make more sense to have an appointed friend take your pooch home or to someone else's house right after the vows.

SWEET AND LOW: *Choosing Your Cake*

There's a rumor going around that, once upon a time in a land called Chelsea, boys didn't eat cake. Rules, like those boys, are made to be broken, and cake is a fun and fantastic part of any wedding celebration. The cake (or cakes) symbolizes your commitment to each other. In olden days, the husband would hit the bride over the head with a bun; the crumbs meant she was fertile (and people think gay guys have kinky habits!).

Regardless of tradition, cakes are fabulously fun and très chic. The varieties are as numerous as the calories: from organic to red velvet to cupcakes to cheesecake to carrot cake to basic chocolate. Give your wedding a Marie Antoinette go and order away. It does need to be pointed out that a cake is not required, and you have every etiquette right to leave it off the menu. If you do decide to nix the flour, notify guests ahead of time. If not, you might end up with so many queries you'll be left with egg on your face.

STAR SEARCH

Talk to restaurants where the desserts are fantastic, and see if their baker does weddings. Ask friends, relatives, and all vendors. • Never assume a baker can make a cake in the shape of Jake Gyllenhaal's face; ask to see pictures of previous custom cakes. • Cake toppers are optional; if you prefer an inscription or nothing at all, by all means have your cake and leave it alone, too. • Cake refrigeration on the day of your wedding is a must; if you're having a cake delivered, make sure the site has proper facilities. • The baker should deliver the cake on the day of your ceremony. If he or she can't, you're going to have to find someone who can pick it up, store it, and set it up. • The cake, unlike your ex, can't be old and stale. It should be baked no more than a day before the wedding.

WHAT EVERY 'MO NEEDS TO KNOW

Some caterers supply the cakes, some don't, and some give you the option of going in-house or ordering your own. If you want something extra creative, or if the caterer or restaurant you've booked doesn't specialize in sweets, seek out a cake maker on your own. • Many guests won't eat cake, so you don't need to go overboard. Fifty slices for 50 guests is adequate. • The dessert course is optional if you're having a cake; think about what kind of eaters you're having, and how much money you want to save or spend. • Lots of people are allergic to nuts, so keep that in mind when ordering the Peanut M&M'S® seven-layer cake. • If you provide your own cake, some sites will demand a cake-cutting fee; find out how much, and decide if it's worth it to bring your own. • Shoving filling in your husband's mouth is not nearly as cute as you think — save it for the honeymoon, boys!

STRAIGHT TALK

In addition to the regular cake, a groom's cake is common. It is generally a different flavor than the main cake, and is served separately. Sometimes, the groom's cake is packaged in boxes and given to guests upon their exit. While a groom's cake used to be in the shape of something "manly" (a football, a race car), and in a chocolate flavor, now it is pretty much served in any shape and taste.

THE MAN DIFFERENCE

Ironically, the groom's cake is not that common in gay weddings, since nowadays one cake fits all. Cake pairings are still very big, with something like carrot cake next to a more traditional cake. Don't think because you're "guys" that people will frown on you if you get the big white cake with the fancy toppers. On the contrary, they'll think it's as sweet as the two of you.

IF YOU KNEW HE WAS COMING . . .

Baking your own cake is a wonderful idea for a small, casual wedding, especially if you, or someone close to you, is a terrific cook. Think twice, however, if the guest list is over 100. Not only do you have to factor in time, you need to worry about storage, refrigeration, and even transportation.

HAVING YOUR TOP AND SAVING IT, TOO

There's a custom of saving the top tier of the cake for your one-year anniversary. Problem is, freezer burn is likely to set in. You might want to cheat a bit and dig in on your one-month anniversary or any other special day.

SPEED DATES

If your cake is not a high priority, or if it's a simple confection, you can put off ordering it until about four months prior to the wedding. If you're clueless about cakes, your baker should offer you several suggestions. He or she will then arrange a cake-tasting date, so you can eat up and narrow down.

$$

CHEAP TRICKS

It's as old as your own trick days: have a small, gorgeous, tiered cake to present to guests, and a sheet cake in the back that the caterers cut up and serve to everybody. • Keep those layers to a minimum; every "floor" costs more, so stay away from the tiers. • Wrap up cakes as favors; it's an idea guests can sink their teeth into. • It's worth repeating that, if you're having a cake, you can skip the dessert course. You'll save money — and calories.

THESE ARE A FEW OF MY LOVED ONES' 'FAVOR'ITE THINGS: *Shopping for Favors*

Favors are a sweet touch that says "thanks for coming" to all your guests, and they serve as the wedding version of the Oscar® gift bag — something to surprise your "stars" with as they exit the site. Of course, as has been mentioned previously, favors aren't required, and cutting them out is a great way to save money. Should you want to have favors, think outside the box of matches. Favors styles and prices run the gamut, from fortune cookies to Champagne flutes to DIY baked goods. Gay-specific favors are easily found online, as are pretty much every favor idea under the sun. Before you splurge, go over that guest list carefully, and do the math. The only "rule" when it comes to favors is to make sure every guest gets one, and to try to make the gift something people won't throw away on their way out the door.

PRESENT TENSE: *Gifts for the Wedding Couple and the Wedding Party*

Everyone in your wedding party receives a gift, including flower girls and ring bearers — if your dog serves as an usher, we'll leave that choice up to you. If you are only having one attendant for each of you, the task is pretty simple. Spend however much you think is wise, and make sure the two of you coordinate prices. Your best man or woman shouldn't receive a $3,000 spa certificate if his attendant gets an iTunes coupon. The gifts do not have to be the same, but the price and level of formality should be consistent.

If there are more attendants, it's best to choose the same item, if only to avoid a "who got the better deal?" exchange. Plus, it's easier on you. People go lavish or lax; there is no set rule. Since your attendants will be getting you a gift, keep the formality of your

wedding in mind, as well as your registry. If your affair is being held in St. Patrick's Cathedral (first of all, good luck with that!), and nothing on your registry costs less than $10,000, give gifts that match the occasion. Mothers usually get corsages in lieu of gifts.

ON THE RECEIVING END

The rumor that guests should spend the same amount of money on a gift that you're spending on them — the meal, etc. — is ludicrous. A wedding is not a 50/50 exchange between the hosts and the hosted. Make sure people know that you view any gift they give you as a wonderful token of their love.

$$

CHEAP TRICKS

In this case, it's each one of you. If you're looking to save some money, opt out of your gifts to each other, or put it off till a later date. Make an agreement that you'd rather spend that money elsewhere, and stick to it. This isn't the time to say "no gifts," then surprise him with a new car for your honeymoon getaway. He'll be so embarrassed that all he'll want to do is run away from you.

CHAPTER 8: FIVE MONTHS AHEAD
WHEELING & DEALING

- [ ] Book your personal wedding transportation
- [ ] Purchase rings
- [ ] Finalize details with each vendor
- [ ] Firm up all travel plans
- [ ] Fill out all change of address and name-change forms
- [ ] If necessary, hire an event planner or designer
- [ ] Go through all electronic calendars and delete your exes; ass-dialing at five months is not cool

If you've ever found yourself saying, "Wasn't it just summer last week?" as you're bundling up in winter clothes, you know how quickly time flies. The five-month mark means you're more than halfway there, and it's time to buckle down and get in gear. It's all the more fitting that transportation kicks in now, as you're driving to that finish line. This is also the month of checklists: checking on the flowers, checking on the menu, checking the registry, and keeping in check any drama — yours or anyone else's. Remember to relax and enjoy the chaos; it's a beautiful storm.

LOCO MOTION: *Booking Your Transportation*

One way or another, you have to get to your ceremony and reception sites. If your event is being held at your home, this is one area that you don't need to worry about, right? Not necessarily. In addition to getting any attendants to your home, you also have to decide how you're exiting your affair. Transportation is yet another area of wedding planning that can cost virtually nothing (your

backyard site is followed by the two of you walking down the nearby nature trail) or can break the bank (you just couldn't resist leaving in a hot-air balloon). It's not what you do that matters, it's how you get there from here.

STRAIGHT TALK

Following tradition from times of yore, the bride arrives at the ceremony site with her father and attendants. The husband arrives with his best man — and pays for it.

THE MAN DIFFERENCE

Tradition blows. Arrive any which way pleases you, in any fashion of your choice. For convenience's sake, it's great to provide transportation for all members of the wedding, and it's a perfect chance to get the party started. You and the groom can arrive together, with party members in another car, and parents or close relatives in another. If your wedding is being held on a beautiful summer day and you want to walk, go ahead. But make an alternate plan in case of rain. And do remember that long walks mean lots of sweat and sweaty clothing.

WHAT EVERY 'MO NEEDS TO KNOW

Stretch limos hold about 12 people, regular limos hold about six, and town cars are like cabs — think about four guests. You can rent vans or even buses for the party, and everything from horse-drawn carriages to motorcycles for the two of you. • If you rent a limo, don't assume the pretty one you saw on the lot is yours; specify the model and color in the contract. • Make sure you have the name and contact numbers of all drivers (including a landline in case of interference) as well as substitute drivers. The drivers also need to have the appropriate attire to match the formality of your affair. • If you're not big drinkers or don't feel like watching TV the day of your wedding, cut out a lot of the fancy extras that you'll be charged for when renting a limo. • Find out if there's a discount for a certain number of cars, as well as using the same vehicles on the wedding day as you do for the rehearsal dinner and any prewedding parties. • Drivers usually expect a tip, so find out what it is and arrange for someone to take care of it on the wedding day. You also need to know if you're responsible for paying for gas, or if the company takes care of the pumping.

$$

CHEAP TRICKS

Cheap is the new black; colored limos are generally cheaper than basic black, so consider that baby-blue car that matches your baby's blue eyes. • Unless you're superstitious or easily creeped out, check funeral homes for limos; they often have cheaper cars. • Make like Rosa and park it in a bus. You can stash about 50 people inside, and it can be a great way to arrive at a casual affair, especially a beach bash or relaxed outdoor ceremony.

VALET DICTORIAN

Valet service might be provided by your site, or you might have to arrange it yourself. The rule of thumb says you should plan on one person for every five cars. You might be able to hire a few valets to guide the cars into the parking area, like you see at big events. For this type of service, you usually need one valet for every 100 guests.

NEIGHBORHOOD WATCH

Should you be marrying at home, call the town council to find out about any parking restrictions in your area. Also, contact the police to let them know about your event. Perhaps most important, consider inviting your close neighbors, as they'll be less likely to complain about the congestion and the noise if they're the ones making most of it.

SPEED DATE

If transportation is not a huge priority, you can put this off until a month before the wedding. If you have lots of people to move, and a big affair, and it's prom season (March through June), do this ASAP, or it might be like the old days when Mom chauffeured you to your "friend" Billy's house!

(IF YOU LOVE HIM) PUT A RING ON IT: *Bands of Matrimony*

Wedding bands are probably the most personal aspect of your wedding, as they are gifts to last a lifetime. Although it's not essential to purchase your rings at the five-month point (you can wait up to a month before the big day), the sooner you decide on your rings, the more time you'll have to concentrate on last-minute emergencies. By the way, no one is holding a gun to your head (except maybe your groom), forcing you to buy rings now. Some men don't care for jewelry, and some would rather put it off to a later date. As long as you both agree, you're set in stone.

HEAVY METAL? DIFFERENT RING TYPES

There are three basic metal ring types. Silver is the cheapest, and sterling silver (yep, it's what you eat with) is 92.5 percent pure. Next up is gold, with 24 karats being as pure as you are. Fourteen karats is the most commonly used (58.5 percent gold), and you can go down from there. Gold comes in different colors, including pink! Finally, platinum is the strongest of the metals, and more expensive than silver or gold rings.

STRAIGHT TALK

Traditionally, the woman sizes up her man's hand, buys her beau a ring, and saves it until the best man hands it to her on the wedding day. Tradition also says that people shouldn't sleep together till their wedding night, and that's like paying for a day pass at Disney World® without knowing what the rides are like.

THE MAN DIFFERENCE

Shopping for rings is probably one of the most fun things two guys can do with each other in public. Feel free to choose your rings together, or, if you prefer, make it a surprise. The problem with the latter idea is that he may just hate the damn thing and end up at Vinnie's Pawn Shop two days before your wedding. (I jest, of course; he'll probably wait until *after* the wedding.) Also, many jewelers will tell you it's important to try on the ring and make sure you're comfortable with how it feels before you actually purchase it. But you guys know each other better than anyone else, so go with your heart if you're set on surprising one another.

The moment you picked up this book, you started breaking a lot of rules, so feel free to keep breaking them. If you don't want your rings to match, it's all good. There's no rule that says your rings have to be gold or platinum or have diamonds in them or any other "wedding" tradition. You can spend $200 on a ring or $2,000. It's not a

money thing; it's a matter of commitment. Should you be kooky, crazy, nutty guys, you can even purchase a ring for some place other than your finger. Just be aware that everyone's going to want to see the thing. Good luck explaining that one to Mom!

WHAT EVERY 'MO NEEDS TO KNOW

Be wary of discount jewelry stores. More often than not the "amazing sale" is a markdown from an inflated price. Stick to a reputable dealer. • If you're incorporating a diamond or any other stone, make sure the price includes setting and stone. To keep costs down, keep the setting simple. • Regarding diamonds: no matter what any jeweler tells you, there is no 100 percent way of making sure your purchase is not a "conflict diamond" or "blood diamond," sold to fund a rebellion or civil war in countries all over the world. Your best bet is to look for the Kimberly Process seal on the certificate; it's a certificate of approval from the Gemological Institute of America (GIA).

SPEED DATE

Unless your rings are highly customized, they should be available within two weeks of purchase. Confirm all details ahead of time, so there are no last-minute surprises.

VENDOR MACHINE: *Making Sure All the Elements Are Well Oiled*

Now's the time to do a thorough assessment of all the elements of your wedding. Go through the list of all vendors involved, and schedule and confirm details. (Note: If you hired a real pro, who's on top of his duties, he should keep you posted, but don't leave anything to chance.) By now, you need to make the final decision on flowers, and you need to choose the menu with your caterer. Once that's done, your caterer will give you a deadline for all last-minute changes; make sure you respect his or her work and stick with it. Your band and/or DJ needs to have a playlist, and you have to double-check with your DJ to make sure Katy Perry's "Teenage Dream" is in their collection. Talk to your cake baker about your decisions, and if the tastings haven't begun, schedule the appointments. Check your registry to make sure it's updated. Add more items if you need to; you can even register at another place if you think the one store is too limited. If there is any ambiguity with a vendor, or an element that has not been decided or hammered out and placed in a contract, do it now.

PARTY ON?

If your friends and family are clueless about parties, talk to at least one of them about arranging events. They could be waiting for a signal from you or your fiancé, or they may just not be sure who's doing what. As stated before, you don't "decide" on parties or who hosts, but this is the 21st century, and you're two men. Always allow people to throw you the parties of their dreams, and also feel free to give anyone a push or a few conceptual details about the type of bash you'd like.

Fit to Be Tied

MONTH 5 — Important fact: absolutely no one cares about your body as much as you do, and that includes the guy by your side. Own it. Work it. And love it!

—*Joey Gonzalez*

TRAVELER'S CHECK: *Prepping for Your Trip*

Firm up all travel plans. Book all flights and hotels, and make sure your documents are in order. This is also a good time to bone up on your destination, whether with guidebooks of Greece or Hemingway's *A Moveable Feast* for your trip to Paris. Make sure your wardrobe is ready, and check that you've got all the stylish luggage you need — don't assume it'll show up three days before your wedding just because it's on your registry list.

HOME ADVANTAGE: *Taking Care of Business*

A good chunk of you probably live together, and don't have many changes in regard to your postwedding life — see how much simpler it is for gays to get married? If you are moving in with him or you're both moving to a new home, take care of the basics. Complete change-of-address notifications, throw out or donate items from your current residence, and, if you've taken a new last name, make sure your bills and other correspondence reflect that change. If you haven't discussed finances by now, well, you probably need to go back a few months — or years. Decide how you're going to divvy up credit cards and bank accounts. Some couples opt for joint and individual accounts, especially when there are separate businesses involved. A wedding book shouldn't serve as a financial adviser, only a helpful reminder to check your balances.

DESIGN ON YOUR DIME: *When You Need Event Planners*

If people start asking you, "Who's your designer?" don't panic and think you missed a crucial wedding-planning step. Designers and event planners are a little like wedding planners, but more specific. They also add a good chunk of change to your budget.

Generally, a designer is someone you hire to carry out a detailed, and difficult, theme. For instance, if you're set on having an Egyptian-themed barge wedding — on a barge, no less — you're probably going to need a bit more help than you can get from 1-800-FRUGALRUS. Designers can redo an entire building to suit your specific theme, or add amazing touches, like bringing in acrobats or fire-eaters, or adding dramatic elements like ice bars or an on-site casino. You can hire event planners and designers for some special details, or have them take complete charge of your affair. Ask around, and make sure you see tons of examples of their work. And take a good hard look at what the guy you interview is wearing. If he looks like a lion tamer, he's going to turn your wedding into a circus.

PROPOSITION GR8?

One morning as I was heading to work, I was waiting for the elevator, and Andy was waiting for me at the apartment door. I described to him my fears that the door to marriage was closing upon us, in a symbolic way, "just like the elevator," and that we might just want to go to Connecticut and get married while it was still an option. As the doors were closing, I heard Andy say, "Okay." In the elevator I thought, "That was the most half-assed, unromantic marriage proposal ever."

—JOHN, MARRIED TO ANDY, NEW YORK, 2011

CHAPTER 9: FOUR MONTHS AHEAD
SUIT YOURSELF

- ☐ Choose your formalwear, for you and your male attendants
- ☐ Hire hair stylists and makeup artists
- ☐ Think how much fun it would be to surprise your new groom with a mustache — *after* the wedding
- ☐ Finalize your guest list
- ☐ Brush off that tuxedo you wore to your senior prom and pat yourself on the back for keeping it all these years — now throw it away

E verybody loves a sharp-dressed man, everybody wants to dance and sing, and everybody wants to rule the world of their wedding. So let's turn the songs of your heart into reality. At the four-month mark, you get to concentrate on what really matters — *you*. Decide on your outfits, groom yourself, and get ready for your close-up. The wedding, this thing that probably once seemed as alien as Sigourney Weaver battling monsters in space, is becoming reality, and take it for all it's worth. Because, most of all, everybody is a star.

OUT OF THE CLOSET: *Formalwear Choices*

If one of you is wearing a white wedding dress and the other a tux, then you've got your style scheme figured out. If not, it's time to make some decisions. While it's simple enough to rent or buy matching tuxes (and there's nothing wrong with that choice), many of you will want to complement each other, rather than go for identical attire. Talk to any stylist and they'll suggest outfits that work together, yet keep you from turning into those clones you used to hang out with in Chelsea.

TOPS AND BOTTOMS

The formality and time of your wedding will play a big part in how you dress, as will the season and venue. Like many a bride, men are now changing into different outfits: a formal look for the ceremony and a more casual getup for the reception. To help you find the look of love, here are some ideas on various formalwear options:

Tuxedo Junction. The most basic tuxedo is the one you probably already wore when you were "straight" and took that girl you "got to second base with" to the prom. The only rule regarding tuxedos is that they shouldn't be worn unless the affair is after 6 p.m. You can go with a peak lapel, a notch, or a shawl. Also, you don't need to go black, even if the affair is "black tie." You can wear a gray tux, but stay away from a tuxedo that's rainbow colored.

One of the other common tuxedo types is the "white tie," in which the suit has a long tailcoat with no buttons, and a top hat and cane — think Fred Astaire in those great Hollywood musicals. You don't see this look often, except for very formal affairs. A "stroller" is worn before 6 p.m. and is accompanied by pinstriped trousers. It's longer than a regular tuxedo jacket and usually a different color than black. The "cutaway," or "morning coat," also has a long black tail and is accompanied by striped trousers and a waistcoat. Once again, the garment is usually reserved for formal, morning affairs.

Suiting Up. It's becoming more common for men to go tuxless at their affairs, so by all means check out the alternatives. Semiformal affairs call for khakis and linen shirts, with matching sandals, natch! Evening affairs can mean gorgeous, complementing suits. As for bow ties, it's another area in which people are straying from the traditional path. (Class note: if you do wear a bow tie, make sure it's a real one —

someone can tie it for you.) Couples are opting for ties ("four-in-hand," in wedding lore). Whatever you do wear dictates the fashion for the rest of the party, so if you've decided to have your nuptials in matching jockstraps, say it on the leather-press invitations.

Cumbersome Buns. Cummerbunds aren't nearly as popular as they once were, and are more commonly replaced by vests. If you opt for the bunds, but don't know which way is up, think of their nickname, "crumb catchers"; the pleats go upward so as to catch any wayward food particles.

Straight Jackets? The Rest of the Party. Assuming your guys need tuxes, it's wise to pick a formalwear-rental store near the wedding destination. Most companies will offer free measurements in the hometown of guests. Unlike women's garments, which are ordered ahead of time, the guys should be able to pick up their rentals the day before the wedding. Make sure they have time to try them on. A missing shirt can be replaced, but pants that are two inches too short can't be fixed. (Speaking of shirts, it's a smart idea to bring extras in a similar design — you never know when disaster, or red wine, might strike.)

LOVE GENDER: Transgender Choices

You can't talk about gay weddings without discussing transgender ceremonies, even if the subject could, well, go either way. If you're a guy in a relationship with a transgendered man, the legal-marriage laws vary in each state (as they do for all transgender marriage). Your wedding, on the other hand, will only be affected by how your friends and family perceive your relationship.

If you're a man, and your spouse is now a woman, is this the right book to pick up, or should you be looking at mainstream bridal publications? There's also a chance that your new husband is recently gay, as heterosexual women get sex changes in the same way that straight men do.

Whomever you turn to for wedding advice depends on your personal needs and preference. If you need a bridal dress but don't feel comfortable reading *Red-State Weddings*, or are uneasy at a traditional bridal shop, hit the vintage shops or a more casual wedding store, such as David's Bridal. (FYI: Your new sexuality is something that everyone should embrace, so please hit every couture shop on the planet, should that be your wish.) Like so many brides, you can also browse through regular department stores. One point worth mentioning is that, for transgender brides, the shoulders and hips will probably be larger than other women's. Consider A-line dresses and forgo the shoulder pads!

Shoe Story. Shoes aren't included with the price of a tux, and the guys need to know that there'll be an additional fee. If you feel comfortable with them going their own way, allow them to put their own best foot forward.

Remember, you're not required to pay for the attendants' clothing, but if you'd like to help out, it's a great way to say thank you. Make sure the party knows that you're paying, so they don't stare at the expensive tux and worry about whether it's going to max out their credit card.

In Sync. If you're not wearing tuxes, let the attendants know what you *are* wearing, so they can pick out something that fits your style. If monochrome is the theme for the evening, you don't want your best man in rainbow stripes. The grooms should stand out by coordinating their outfits in one style and/or color (say, gray), and having the other guys in something slightly different. If you're all wearing boutonnieres, yours should be slightly more prominent, often with an extra bloom. When in doubt about any wedding fashion, ask the salesperson.

Speed Dates: Four months ahead of the wedding gives you plenty of time to figure out your fashion statements. If you're donning tuxes, and are having your ceremony during prom season (March through June), try to get on this a bit earlier.

$$

CHEAP TRICK
If you want to wear tuxes, think twice before buying the garments. Yes, every guy should have a tuxedo, but if your weight fluctuates and your business doesn't require attending many formal events, it might not be worth the expense.

PROPOSITION GR8

For years I had gay friends celebrate their relationships with a commitment ceremony of some sort, which I thought was terrific. But for me — and I stress, for ME — a ceremony that had no legal status wasn't something that held any interest. If I was going to do this, I wanted it to be legal.

In the fall of 2003, I was headed to Toronto with the national touring company of *Chicago*, the musical, for a month. My "boyfriend" (as a 40-something man, I don't care for that word, by the way) of nine years, Michael, had never been to Toronto, so he was coming out to visit. Marriage equality had recently became a reality for Ontario. So, pretty calmly, I asked Michael on the phone, "Do you want to get married?" Since there would be an actual marriage license, I felt it carried the kind of "authority" that fit my definition of being "legal."

Before Michael arrived in Toronto, I headed down to city hall and picked up the marriage-license application. Even though the concept was new to the people working there, no one looked at me oddly in even the slightest way. The woman behind the counter could not have been nicer or more kind.

One note about the license application: since the law was new, the applications had not been rewritten. There were two spaces for names: Bride and Groom. Since I picked up the application, I put my name in the Groom column, making Michael the "Bride." Michael joked about that often.

On October 17, 2003, nine years to the day that Michael and I met, we were legally married in Toronto by Senior Justice Lauren Marshall. Justice Marshall was very kind, and took great care and time allowing us to take in the joy of this important moment in our lives. It really is amazing, when the time comes to say "I do," how much weight that moment carries.

Just two friends from *Chicago* came as our witnesses. This wasn't for anyone but Michael and me. Just us and two words: I do.

A few years later, right before the 2008 election, we decided to get married again during the time the window remained open for gay couples to marry in California. A week before the election, with polls indecisive about Prop 8, we headed to Palm Springs. And on a very busy Friday afternoon at Palm Springs City Hall, we renewed our vows — this time under the auspices of the state of California.

Again, everyone at city hall was kind, warm, and supportive. All of the city council members had the authority to marry couples, and with time ticking toward the election, couples and families were lined up in the city hall lobby waiting for their turn. Spirits were high everywhere in the building. Ceremonies were taking place in the city council chamber, meeting rooms, the mayor's office . . . you name it, someone was saying "I do" somewhere.

Married by the mayor, the small quiet ceremony was just as powerful the second time. Now in our 18th year together, I love that I use the word "husband" every day when I reference Michael in conversation.

Michael and I are one of the 18,000 couples in California who retain our married status. I feel a little special but sad about that. Everyone should have the right to marry the person he or she loves. I look forward to the day when all marriage is treated the same everywhere.

— RANDY SLOVACEK, MARRIED TO MICHAEL CAPRIO FOR THE FIRST TIME IN TORONTO, CANADA, 2003

GROOM GROOMING: *Looking Stylish*

And you thought women were tough. Guys want to look fantastic on their wedding day, and that often means lavishing lots of extra attention on their better halves — i.e., their right or left profile. But seriously, guys are hiring hairstylists for their weddings, spending money on personal trainers, and going on a lot of smart (and crazy) diets. Don't do anything rash. Follow a few simple rules so you can put your best face forward.

HAIR SHORT CUTS

Hair plays an important part for all grooms, and consult a stylist if you feel it's needed — and you can afford it. (Keep in mind your female attendants and moms, too. If you want to treat them to a hair stylist or makeup artist, book now. Great stylists will always do a practice run ahead of time, and then show up on the day of the wedding.) Regarding your own look, if you've decided to let your hair grow out for the ceremony, or do anything drastic — like shave it off — try it now. Errors can be fixed four months ahead of time, not four hours ahead of time. If you wax any part of your body, stick to the schedule you're on. Do not get your first bikini wax a day before the wedding. You're going to break out a lot more than that darling Speedo. The same goes for plucking your brows — if your skin isn't used to it, you'll get acne.

BODY LANGUAGE

Tattoos are all the rage, and if you get "His" and "His" tattooed on your butts, they will be there for good — and Mom's going to want to see it. Anything extreme, including piercings, needs to be discussed with your partner and carefully considered. Tattoos take time to properly heal, and they're (surprise!) painful. Once again, not something you run out and try at the bachelor party. Teeth whitening, too, needs to be discussed with your dentist. You might find your smile to be a bit too dazzling at first, so plan it ahead of time. Many over-the-counter whitening products work great for stain brushups.

PRETTY AND PINK

Last-minute pampering is wonderful to ease stress and give you that extra zing before the wedding. Massages are great, but you're not going to have time on your wedding day. Plan it the day before, and bring the Mr. along. A pedicure, too, should be done beforehand. Facials can lead to mild breakouts, so aim for a few weeks ahead. Try to schedule manicures the day before the wedding — you want those hands to look as polished as you do — but the wedding day is not the time to rush off to a salon. As for Botox, if you haven't already, don't go there.

Fit to Be Tied

MONTH 4 — Take your fat for a run (or a bicycle ride, or a swim, for 30 minutes every other day), then ditch it when nobody is looking.

—*Joey Gonzalez*

Chapter 10: Three Months Ahead
CONGRATULATIONS ON 90 DAYS!

- [ ] Write your vows
- [ ] Ask friends and relatives to speak at your ceremony
- [ ] Take dance lessons
- [ ] Accept the fact that you will never be as good a dancer as Fred Astaire — or even Fred Mertz
- [ ] Think about how to deal with major mishaps
- [ ] Create a wedding emergency kit

It's worth a token of some sort. You've made it this far, and you've only got a few more months till you hit the big day. There has been drama (he wants "My Heart Will Go On" for the first dance; you want "Man, I Feel Like a Woman"), and high drama (your wedding date coincides with the season finale of *The Voice*), but you're staying afloat on the sometimes turbulent waters. Now's the time to get a wee bit personal and start thinking about the little things. In addition to something old, something new, something borrowed, and something blue, pinpoint the other, finer things you want in your wedded life.

SMALL TALK: *Writing Those Vows*

It's never easy to say what's in your heart. Add the pressure of a wedding, and writer's block is understandable. Never fear: the only requirement for ceremony vows is that they be truthful. If you want to keep vows short and sweet, wonderful (and your guests might thank you). Just make sure you're both on the same brief page. Traditional

vows are yours to honor, and your officiant can help you choose the most appropriate words. "Till death do us part" and "in sickness and in health" aren't all that big anymore in heteroville, so feel free to leave them out. Although it's nice to keep your vows from your husband until the wedding day, consider going over ideas and lengths, and how much sentiment you want in comparison to light humor.

DULY NOTED

Experts are mixed about holding pieces of paper for vows (ditto toasts from friends), and it does take away the spontaneity. However, if the only way you're going to remember anything but his name — or if even that is iffy — by all means go ahead and write it down. If Meryl does it for acceptance speeches, you can do it for matrimonial pledges.

SPEAK NOW OR FOREVER HOLD YOUR PIECE OF PAPER

If you want friends or relatives to speak, now's the time to approach them. (Also, be prepared for people to ask you if they can do a reading, and have your response ready. If your brother Bob wants to say a few words, there's a good chance your groom's brother Rob will feel left out if not approached.) Speakers can recite poems, including their favorite sonnets, sections of books, or their own words. Nothing is off-limits, but if your best man wants to act out "I'm Sexy and I Know It," you need to make sure the officiant thinks it's appropriate for the formality of the wedding.

YOU SHOULD BE DANCING?

Not necessarily. It's wonderful to surprise your guests with a gutsy first-dance tango, but if you've got two left feet or would just rather concentrate on other elements of your wedding, you just may want to nip that idea in the bud. Dance classes are easily available, and ballroom has taken off big-time due to *DWTS*. You can search for classes, and even purchase DVDs. If you're both pros, or determined, take those lessons now. Everything is harder in front of an audience (remember your brief porn career?), and nerves will mean you've got to rehearse your asses off — literally.

GROUND CONTROL TO MAJOR MISHAPS:
Everything That Might Go Wrong and How to Deal

Now that the pieces of your wedding are coming together, it's good to spend a little time analyzing some of the more common wedding-day snafus, and ways to solve them. (Problem Solver Number One: As long as the two of you are there, nothing is extreme enough to spoil the day.)

FAMILY EMERGENCY

Unfortunately, people do get ill, and they can't always plan their illness around your wedding date. If a parent or close loved one can't attend the wedding, it's time to make some quick decisions. The worst-case scenario is that you postpone the wedding. Yes,

you will lose a lot of money and will have to make a lot of concessions. You need to talk to everyone involved — including, if possible, the ill person — and determine the best course. You can always have a small ceremony, make a toast in the absent loved one's honor, and then plan a larger reception later on. If there is a death in the immediate family, canceling the wedding is usually the most common recourse. As long as you go with your heart, you'll do the right thing. If you or your groom are ill, there are ways that you can adjust your ceremony to make the stress easier. No one's going to complain if you're forced to be seated during the ceremony because you've got a 102-degree fever. You can skip the first dance, and take a seat with the crowd. People will have to approach you during the reception, but they will understand your predicament.

LATE FOR AN IMPORTANT DATE

Gridlock happens, and among the people that might show up late to your ceremony or reception are the officiant, florists, caterers, wedding-party members, DJ or band, photographer or videographer, and you. (In other words, everyone.) Savvy do-it-yourself planners are quick on their feet. If food doesn't show up, order takeout. Seriously. If flowers aren't there, try to make do with what's at the site, joke about it, and scrounge up some last-minute blooms. If there's no DJ or band yet, talk to the site to see if they have music available. This is also the time to grab someone's iPod and hook it up. Cakes can be purchased at local bakeries, and someone can run out to a liquor store and buy some bottles of Champagne until the bartender arrives. If your best man or woman or important attendant isn't there, grab someone else and have him or her do the honors. If your officiant is tardy, try to cover all of the other elements of the ceremony until he or she arrives. You can always recite your vows at the reception site. It's imperative that you have all cell phone and landline numbers, and have trusted attendants who can make emergency runs.

THE SEWING KIT AND CABOODLE

A trusted friend or relative should keep a box of essentials: sewing matcrials, Band-Aids®, aspirin, stain remover, Kleenex®, socks, T-shirts, a first-aid kit, and anything else you think might come in handy. Red-wine stains are a bitch, so consider keeping away from the dark stuff until the reception is in full swing. If your clothes get badly stained or torn during the reception, all the more reason for having another outfit in the changing room.

WEATHER OR NOT

It isn't just rain you need to be prepared for. A snowstorm or excessive heat or cold can put a damper on those perfect plans. Even hurricanes or other natural disasters can disrupt your event. Know your weather patterns, and make alternate preparations. Most people avoid, say, the Bahamas in hurricane season, but it's very hard to find a place that's 100 percent safe. Whatever Mother Nature throws at you, have a game plan. This can be anything from quickly bringing a ceremony indoors if it's unseasonably cold (or hot) to moving the reception to a site that's not threatened by tropical storms, or finding a spot that, unlike your backyard, has air-conditioning.

LIONS AND TIGERS AND BADLY BEHAVING BEARS, OH MY!

Unfortunately, not everyone who attends your wedding is going to be the pillar of good manners, and you need to accept this fact of civilization. Around the three-month point is when you're going to find out that Aunt Needie has gone on a hunger strike because she wasn't invited to the wedding; your best friend from high school, Sally Fertile, simply can't leave her triplets at home even though it's an Adults Only affair; and your best man decided to skip the wedding because he's developed love handles. Yes, these are exaggerations, but human quirks are bound to surface — despite your best efforts to keep everything on track. Uninvited guests and unreasonable guests are best dealt with firmly but diplomatically. If you're not getting anywhere with reason, you might have to suck it up and accept distractions. If uninvited tots show up on the day of your wedding, don't kick them out — do the best you can with what you have. If you need to find a replacement attendant, either start calling friends or figure out if you can deal without. And if your meddling relative is that insistent on coming to your wedding, let her. Otherwise, she'll make your heavenly wedding a living hell.

THE EX FACTOR

Folks have mixed feelings about whether or not they should invite their exes. There's no rule about it, so decide for yourself, with your fiancé of course. Don't invite an ex just because you want to be "nice." Consider your hubby's feelings and how it might affect the wedding. Keep in mind, too, that your ex might not want to attend your wedding, but might feel obligated if he receives an invitation. If you're on good enough terms, call him and discuss it ahead of time. Should you have any major doubts, it's usually a sign that you should just say no.

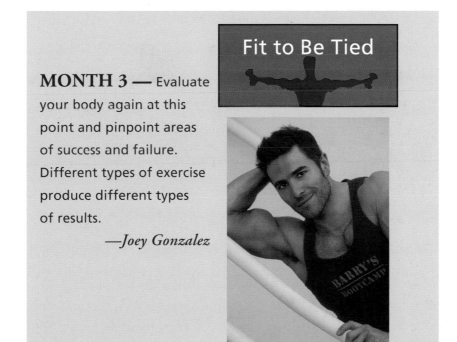

Fit to Be Tied

MONTH 3 — Evaluate your body again at this point and pinpoint areas of success and failure. Different types of exercise produce different types of results.

—*Joey Gonzalez*

Chapter 11: Two Months Ahead
EQUAL RITES

- [ ] Create programs for the ceremony
- [ ] Make or order table cards and place cards
- [ ] Plan some alone time with supportive parents — you'll be too busy in a few weeks
- [ ] Help your moms choose outfits
- [ ] Accept the fact that, yes, you've done everything wrong and your wedding will be a complete disaster
- [ ] Now that you've gotten that tantrum out of the way, continue planning your amazing day!

Whether or not you've dreamed all your life (or just for the past year) of marrying the guy next to you, the fantasy is turning into reality. In addition to all the last-minute arrangements and double-checking and rethinking and stress, you get to sit back and enjoy the work it took to get here. Spend time together talking about and laughing at all the insanity surrounding your wedding, and know that, for the most part, the aggravation you experience will provide great sentimental joy upon reflection. It's time to put the final pieces of the puzzle together and get ready for the perfect fit.

THE MAIN EVENT: *Programs and Places*

Put together the program for your ceremony, which can be detailed or short. It's nice to list who's reading what, as well as the order and time of the events. Many couples make their own programs; with today's software, it's not complicated. You can also

talk to your stationer about creating something unique. Remember to assign someone to hand out programs at the site.

SITTING PRETTY

Table and place cards need to be figured out. Once again, a stationer can create them, or you can do it yourself. If a creative friend offers to make them as a wedding gift, and his ideas fit your theme, by all means allow him to accessorize your affair. Remember, table cards let guests know where their table is, and are usually placed somewhere near the entrance of the reception. Place cards are on the tables themselves and they let guests know which seat is theirs.

TABLE OF CONTENTS: *Alternative Seating Ideas*

STRAIGHT TALK

At hetero weddings, the bride and groom sit at the head of the main table (or alone at a "sweetheart" table), with a set of parents on either side. Next to them, also on both sides, are the wedding-party members, usually without their dates.

THE MAN DIFFERENCE

For a gay wedding, it's more common to dispense with traditional table arrangements and try something a bit more user-friendly. Wedding couples can opt to have a main table, or head table, with the parents on each side, followed by attendants. One problem with this seating arrangement is that attendants often end up sitting away from their partners. Also, you may not have the blessing of both sets of parents. A popular alternative is to keep all wedding-party members close to your main table, then disperse people throughout the reception site. His best man and your best man don't have to be at the same table. Always make sure parents are close to you — and don't play favorites with relatives. Mixing up the crowd, while making sure you don't place feuding uncles at the same spot, creates a nice sense of diversity and allows for guests to mingle with people they don't see every day.

In your rush to create the perfect day, there's probably a couple of older men and women who are just as thrilled as you are. Assuming your parents are behind your nuptials, make sure that you take them aside and spend some personal time with them. Not only are their sons getting married, they're getting married in a way that is new and challenging and probably something your parents didn't expect when you were a tot. This is a perfect time to take moms out to lunch or dinner; ditto dads. You can all go on one outing, or you can spend some real alone time with each one. Let them know how much you appreciate their acceptance and their love.

Out (fitting) Your Moms. Your parents want to look stellar on your wedding day, and who better to help them shop but their gay sons?! Some mothers will have picked their dress 20 years ago, while others might not have a clue as to what to wear. A lot of eyes are going to be on the mothers of the grooms, so make sure they're thrilled with their selections. Don't just brush this step off as something she can take care of, even if she's been to 17,000 weddings. Sit down with her, shop with her, discuss colors with her, and smother her with affection. She's going to be so touched by your attention that you'll feel like you've been born again.

Fit to Be Tied

MONTH 2 — Exercise one hour a day, five days a week, 52 weeks a year. That's only two percent of your time, so quit whining.

—*Joey Gonzalez*

PROPOSITION GR8

Marriage became possible for us in late 2008, when it became legal in neighboring Connecticut. It became meaningful for us in early 2009, when Governor David Paterson ordered that New York state agencies recognize out-of-state same-sex marriages. And in November 2009, it became urgent when the voters in Maine repealed marriage equality by referendum. The door had been opened to us, and, worried that it might be closed, we decided to act.

The legal contract of marriage was important to us because of the security it affords in New York state, particularly in housing and health care. But the marriage ceremony was essential for us so that our community of family and friends could be present to witness and publicly affirm the sacred and enduring nature of our union. Also, in full honesty, our wedding celebration was imperative because it would be antithetical to our natures, as individuals and as a couple, to forgo such an extraordinary occasion for a party!

—RANDY BETTIS & SEAN DWYER, MARRIED IN STAMFORD, CONNECTICUT, 2010

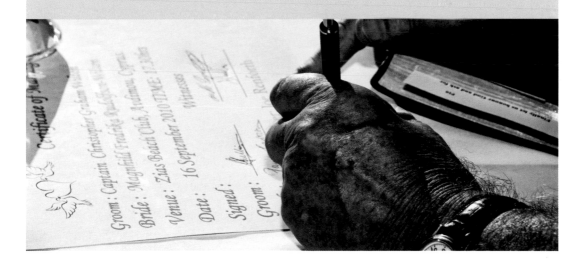

CHAPTER 12: ONE MONTH AHEAD
HAPPY ENDINGS

Since you're one month away from the wedding, it makes the most sense to wrap up this guidebook by counting down the days leading up to your ceremony. Before you start checking off any last-minute items from your list, go through your notes and make sure you haven't forgotten anything major. If there are any big planning steps that have been avoided or neglected, stop everything and take care of them. The one thing that hasn't changed in these 11 months of planning is your love and commitment; even if the wedding doesn't go off without a hitch, the two of you are planned perfection. Eat, drink, celebrate, and feel the love. Congratulations!

FOUR WEEKS BEFORE:

❑ Make sure the seating arrangements are set. Also, verify the final guest count with the caterer and any special dietary needs.

❑ Coordinate vendors. Everyone who's working behind the scenes at your wedding should know one another, and have shared contact information. You should put one reliable person in charge of keeping all the names and numbers, in case of any emergencies. He can be the go-to person and head off disasters.

❑ Update your wedding Web site so that guests know the order of events and have all addresses, information on parties, dress codes, weather conditions, and someone to call if there's a problem.

❑ Address any dress issues. If the females in your wedding party are going formal, make sure they've received their outfits.

❑ Continue mailing out thank-you notes for gifts received.

❑ Check your registry and make last-minute updates. Also, did you double-check to make sure there's a gift table at the reception site?

❑ Start inviting your B-list, if you're getting back a number of "can't attend" RSVPs. Never presume a nonanswer is a negative. Call anyone who hasn't responded — it could be they're lazy, or that they just assume you know they're attending.

❑ Never started that diet regime? Suck it up. It's too late now, and you're only going to wreak havoc on your hormones as well as your tailor.

❑ Keep up that fitness routine — as Joey says. . . .

Fit to Be Tied

MONTH OF THE WEDDING —
Look at yourself naked at least once before you go to sleep. If you're not happy, set your alarm a little earlier — you know what you need to do by now.

—*Joey Gonzalez*

THREE WEEKS BEFORE:

❑ Are the prenuptial parties set? Go over any plans with hosts to make sure one party doesn't coincide with another, and that everyone who needs to be invited has made the cut. Note: Anyone who is invited to a prenuptial party should be on the wedding-guest list. Note, too: Don't force guests to buy you 12 presents. Keep the gift requests to a minimum, and stress to friends that, like life with your new hubby, one package is plenty.

❑ Start checking the weather updates now. If a heavy storm or a massive cold front is headed your way, consider renting that outdoor heater.

❑ If you've hired a stylist for the wedding, book all final appointments and run-throughs.

❑ Contact lodgings where all guests are booked, and confirm. Now's the time to fix up that extra bedroom at home, or contact very good friends about their own living-room sofa, in case someone gets stranded.

❑ Schedule an after-wedding breakfast, brunch, lunch, or cocktail party for guests who will still be in town the day after the wedding. While not mandatory, it's nice if the two of you make an appearance. Put all the information on your Web site, and feel free to e-mail or phone potential attendees, especially if you need an RSVP for the restaurant.

❏ Talk to all participants about ceremony readings and wedding toasts. Make sure they: a) remember that they're doing a reading or toast, and b) know what they're going to say.

❏ Start that teeth-whitening program and any other beauty treatments. Still thinking about growing a mustache for the big day? Forget about it. That's something you should have experimented with back when you were still experimenting.

❏ Still working on those vows? Jot something down. You can edit later. (Feel free to run your words by a close confidant.)

TWO WEEKS BEFORE:

❏ Do your final consultation with vendors to make sure there are no 11th-hour surprises. Answer any questions they still have, and get answers for anything you still don't understand. Clear up any contract disputes or discrepancies. Double-check overtime fees and availability. Find out if the band will play after 10 p.m. if the party escalates, and make sure the bartenders can work past their appointed hour. Know who will be delivering the flowers and cake and when they'll arrive. Ditto the band and DJ, photographer, and videographer. Make sure you have everyone's cell and landline numbers, and make sure they have yours.

❏ If applicable, follow up with newspapers about your wedding announcement.

❑ Take care of going-away business. Have the newspaper and your mail held, find temporary "housing" for your dogs, arrange for a friend to water your plants, and remember to set your DVR to record your favorite shows.

❑ Keep moving stuff into his place or the new house you're both now furnishing — hey, some of those presents from relatives you already opened are going to look wonderful in the new living room. And some of those other presents are going to look great after you return them for something you like! (Oh, yeah, a note on those thank-yous for gifts you aren't nuts about: find a way to politely say how much you're going to enjoy the acid-wash, matching jean jackets, and how shocked you are that Cousin Takky was able to find such a rarity nowadays! And be prepared to have them hanging in your closet when he drops by in his Trans Am.)

❑ Talk to the band and/or DJ about precise musical musts and must-nots. If there's a new hit on the radio you love, or if your grandmother requested a classic, make sure it's accounted for and on the playlist. Double-check with your DJ to confirm that he did not bow to pressure from your sister and bring along a karaoke machine.

❑ Make sure the photographer has a list of must-have shots, and your videographer has a list of what can and cannot be left out.

❑ Subtly remind the wedding party that you do *not* want them to use cans to decorate the back of your getaway car (even though you know that they will). Decide and inform the party if you want bubbles or birdseed for your exit. Also, check with the site about what's allowed and what is not.

ONE WEEK BEFORE:

❑ Make sure all members of the wedding party are clear on their roles. They all need specific directions and times, and a list of events and their duties (readings, etc.). Everyone in the wedding rehearsal needs to know exactly where and when the events will take place.

❑ Update all wedding events for the guests. Post information on your Web site, e-mail details, and call people. Remember, not everyone uses the Internet. Should anyone ask for a list of activities in writing, snail-mail it to them ASAP. And always provide a contact number for last-minute questions and emergencies.

❑ Put together tips and checks, and hand them over to the best man or whoever's in charge, so that payments can be given to the correct people on the day of your wedding.

❑ Pay all your final balances to vendors.

❑ Pick up your tuxes or formalwear. Try them on to make sure everything fits, then put them in garment bags. Though you're no longer in the closet, that's where they should be. Keep spare T-shirts and socks handy for both of you.

❑ Cut your hair and take care of last-minute grooming.

❑ Double-check that you know where the rings are!

❑ Give each other your gifts. Then, relax with your honey by watching a movie (see pages 156–157).

DAY BEFORE:

❑ Get the tuxedos for the gents.

❑ Make sure women have their outfits and that everything fits.

❑ Greet your guests. Make an appearance at all prenuptial parties.

❑ Attend the rehearsal dinner and give attendants their gifts.

❑ Know that, whatever disasters occur, you'll be laughing about them ten years from now.

❑ Get a massage, manicure, and pedicure.

❑ Keep the alcohol intake to a minimum and get to bed at a reasonable hour.

DAY OF:

❑ Love . . .

The Ten Gayest Wedding Movies Evah!

1. Father of the Bride (1950)

WHY IT'S FOR HOMOS: Elizabeth Taylor stars as the blushing bride-to-be. She's every gay boy's dream, of *himself*.

WHY IT'S A FABULOUS FILM: The entire movie is about the preparation for the wedding, told with style, flair, and humor. And Spencer Tracy is terrific as the narrator dad.

WHY YOU MIGHT WANT TO RETHINK COPYING ITS STYLE: Classics are hard to improve on (hence, the less-than-classic remake), and you're probably not wearing a dress. Think of it more as a gift than a guideline.

IMITATION OF LIFE: Have a Liz Taylor movie marathon before your wedding. Start with this one, move on to *Giant*, *Cleopatra*, *Cat on a Hot Tin Roof*, and *Butterfield 8*. Skip *Who's Afraid of Virginia Woolf?*, unless you want ideas on how not to throw a bachelor party.

2. Muriel's Wedding (1994)

WHY IT'S FOR HOMOS: Two words: "ABBA" and, spelled backwards, "ABBA."

WHY IT'S A FABULOUS FILM: Toni Collette plays Muriel, and like so many gay men growing up, she's an outsider who wants to belong.

WHY YOU MIGHT WANT TO RETHINK COPYING ITS STYLE: Do you really want "Dancing Queen" playing 600 times at your reception?

IMITATION OF LIFE: Do the next best thing and throw a *Mamma Mia!* engagement party, complete with outfits, songs, and, if you can swing it, tickets to the show.

3. Bridesmaids (2011)

WHY IT'S FOR HOMOS: It's about bitchy girls preparing for a wedding. Need I say more?

WHY IT'S A FABULOUS FILM: Despite some (literal) toilet humor, it's a touching story about love amid the drama that goes into your wedding. And Wilson Phillips performs at the end!

WHY YOU MIGHT WANT TO RETHINK COPYING ITS STYLE: No matter what variation of party you try, everyone's going to want to re-create the bathroom scene. I smell a flop.

IMITATION OF LIFE: Hire Wilson Phillips. They're available.

4. A Wedding (1978)

WHY IT'S FOR HOMOS: Director Robert Altman sends up an upper-class wedding, with satire, bite, and brilliant humor. What more could you want?

WHY IT'S A FABULOUS FILM: Forty-eight characters make up the story, which involves infidelity, death, and drinks till dawn. Did I mention it's a comedy?

WHY YOU MIGHT WANT TO RETHINK COPYING ITS STYLE: See above.

IMITATION OF LIFE: Watch it before your wedding as a "comfort film." Nothing that happens on your day can possibly be worse than what happens here.

5. The Wedding Banquet (1993)

WHY IT'S FOR HOMOS: A gay man agrees to marry a straight woman for convenience, and, needless to say, it doesn't work as planned.

WHY IT'S A FABULOUS FILM: Love conquers all, and that's what your wedding is all about.

WHY YOU MIGHT WANT TO RETHINK COPYING ITS STYLE: The only beard you want at your wedding is the one you've been trimming all week.

IMITATION OF LIFE: *Brokeback Mountain* director Ang Lee made *The Wedding Banquet*, so, after a viewing of this comedy, move on to our favorite gay cowboys and throw a Country & Western party — your lesbian friends can teach you how to two-step.

6. My Best Friend's Wedding (1997)

WHY IT'S FOR HOMOS: Let's see, Julia Roberts, Cameron Diaz, and Rupert Everett star. All that's missing is some hunky guy like Dermot Mul . . . oh, wait, never mind.

WHY IT'S A FABULOUS FILM: She ends up with her gay best friend . . . just like you.

WHY YOU MIGHT WANT TO RETHINK COPYING ITS STYLE: The two leads think they need to get married by the time they're 28 or they're doomed. Yeah, that'll go over really well with your single daddy friends.

IMITATION OF LIFE: Dionne Warwick music, anyone? Let your friends sing a little prayer for you.

7. The Wedding Singer (1998)

WHY IT'S FOR HOMOS: It takes place in the '80s, and everyone's dressed like Madonna and Cyndi Lauper and George Michael and Boy George. Think any Halloween bash in New York City.

WHY IT'S A FABULOUS FILM: Because the music is from all those people, too. Think any hot club on a Saturday night.

WHY YOU MIGHT WANT TO RETHINK COPYING ITS STYLE: Any mention of an Adam Sandler movie, and your straight male friends might start dancing and imitating his routines — and that's just gonna get ugly.

IMITATION OF LIFE: Everyone loves an '80s party, so get into the groove like it's the very first time.

8. How to Marry a Millionaire (1953)

WHY IT'S FOR HOMOS: Betty Grable, Lauren Bacall, and Marilyn Monroe star. And did you read the title?

WHY IT'S A FABULOUS FILM: Not unlike your Fire Island share, three young girlfriends rent a summer apartment on Sutton Place and scheme their way to the top.

WHY YOU MIGHT WANT TO RETHINK COPYING ITS STYLE: The women are gold diggers until they find love. That's fine, but what gay person actually wants to have a party on Sutton Place?

IMITATION OF LIFE: You can't miss with a Marilyn Monroe pre-wedding movie bash. Start with *Gentlemen Prefer Blondes*, sip your way through *The Seven Year Itch*, and take it on home with *Some Like It Hot*.

9. Four Weddings and a Funeral (1994)

WHY IT'S FOR HOMOS: Upper-crust weddings, British accents, a gay subplot, and Hugh Grant. The Spice Girls couldn't gay-up this film.

WHY IT'S A FABULOUS FILM: Hugh Grant is a cad and a scoundrel who finally finds true love. Remind you of anyone you know?

WHY YOU MIGHT WANT TO RETHINK COPYING ITS STYLE: Did you read the last word in the title?

IMITATION OF LIFE: One wedding might be enough, but a classy countryside engagement is très chic, especially if parasols are included. Nix those nasty British toasts, however. For reasons unknown to everyone, they only sound classy when spoken with an English accent.

10. The Hangover (2009)

Because it's everything you need to know about what *not* to do before your wedding night. Ironically, it's the one film listed here that will make you most happy you're gay.

Index

Page numbers in *italic* refer to practical tips, ways to save money, and frequently asked questions.

Acknowledgments

For this book, all my thanks to the people at Sellers Publishing for taking a chance on me, from Publishing Director Robin Haywood to my editor, Mark Chimsky. It's wonderful in this business to be appreciated. Thanks as well to Managing Editor, Mary Baldwin, and a special debt of gratitude to proofreader Renee Rooks Cooley, and indexer Laura Shelley. I also have to thank Marilyn Allen, from the Allen O'Shea Literary Agency, for basically plucking me from the sky. A big thank you to Melanie Wesslock and Katje Hempel for their amazing photography. And a big smacking kiss (and wedding congratulations) to fitness Superman Joey Gonzalez at Barry's Bootcamp, who can whip my butt into shape any day. And I can't forget my top models, Farhad Zamini and Jorge Horan — just do it, dudes. Special thanks also go to my dear friend Danielle Bobish, at Curtain Up Events, who gives me the best wedding tips ever! Most important for this type of book are the couples who've taken the plunge, told me their stories, braved storms, and sailed blue seas, and who fill me with delight. I hope your honeymoons are forever.

— David Toussaint
www.davidtoussaint.com